Buffy
THE
HIGH SCHOOL YEARS

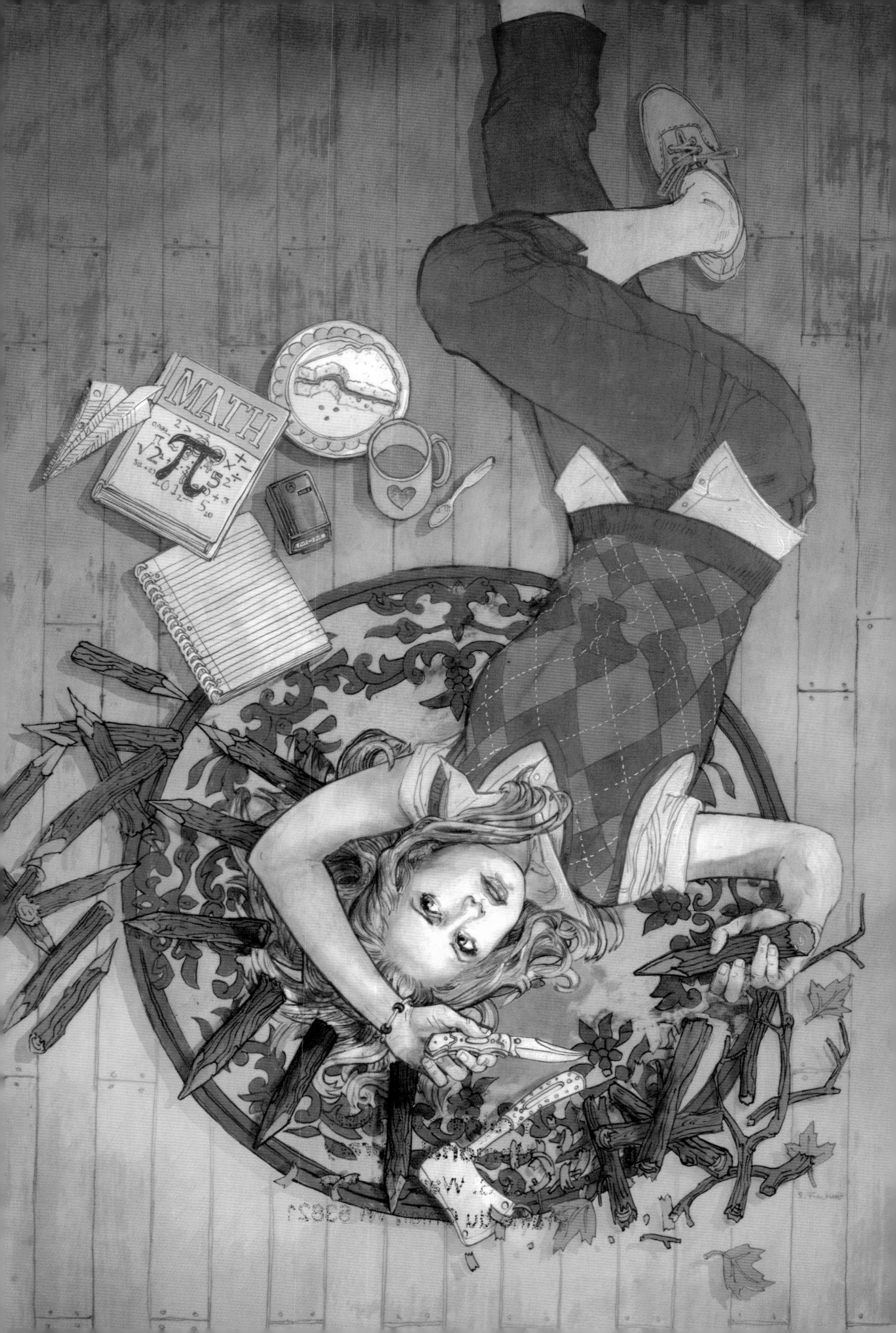
MATH

Buffy
THE HIGH SCHOOL YEARS

PARENTAL PARASITE

SCRIPT
KEL McDONALD

ART
YISHAN LI

COLORS **ROD ESPINOSA**
& TONY GALVAN

LETTERING
RICHARD STARKINGS & COMICRAFT'S
JIMMY BETANCOURT

COVER ART **SCOTT FISCHER**

EXECUTIVE PRODUCER **JOSS WHEDON**

DARK HORSE BOOKS

President & Publisher
MIKE RICHARDSON

Editor
FREDDYE MILLER

Assistant Editor
KEVIN BURKHALTER

Designer
JUSTIN COUCH

Digital Art Technician
CHRISTIANNE GOUDREAU

Special thanks to Nicole Spiegel at Twentieth Century Fox.

This story takes place during *Buffy the Vampire Slayer* Season 1, created by Joss Whedon.

First edition: June 2017　|　ISBN 978-1-50670-304-6　|　10 9 8 7 6 5 4 3 2 1

Published by Dark Horse Books, a division of Dark Horse Comics, Inc.
10956 SE Main Street, Milwaukie, OR 97222　|　DarkHorse.com

Neil Hankerson Executive Vice President · Tom Weddle Chief Financial Officer · Randy Stradley Vice
President of Publishing · Matt Parkinson Vice President of Marketing · David Scroggy Vice President
of Product Development · Dale LaFountain Vice President of Information Technology · Cara Niece
Vice President of Production and Scheduling · Nick McWhorter Vice President of Media Licensing ·
Mark Bernardi Vice President of Book Trade and Digital Sales · Ken Lizzi General Counsel · Dave
Marshall Editor in Chief · Davey Estrada Editorial Director · Scott Allie Executive Senior Editor
· Chris Warner Senior Books Editor · Cary Grazzini Director of Specialty Projects · Lia Ribacchi
Art Director · Vanessa Todd Director of Print Purchasing · Matt Dryer Director of Digital Art and
Prepress · Sarah Robertson Director of Product Sales · Michael Gombos Director of International
Publishing and Licensing

To find a comics shop in your area, call the Comic Shop Locator Service toll-free at (888) 266-4226.
International Licensing: 503-905-2377

Buffy

THE HIGH SCHOOL YEARS

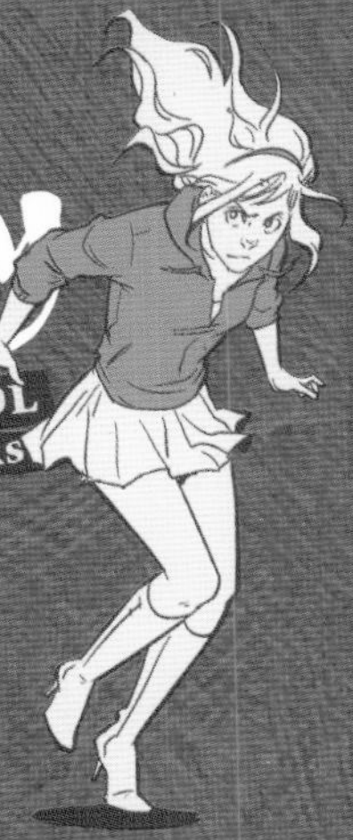

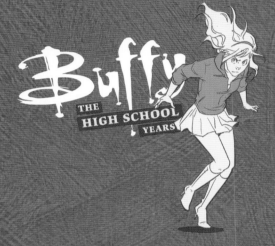

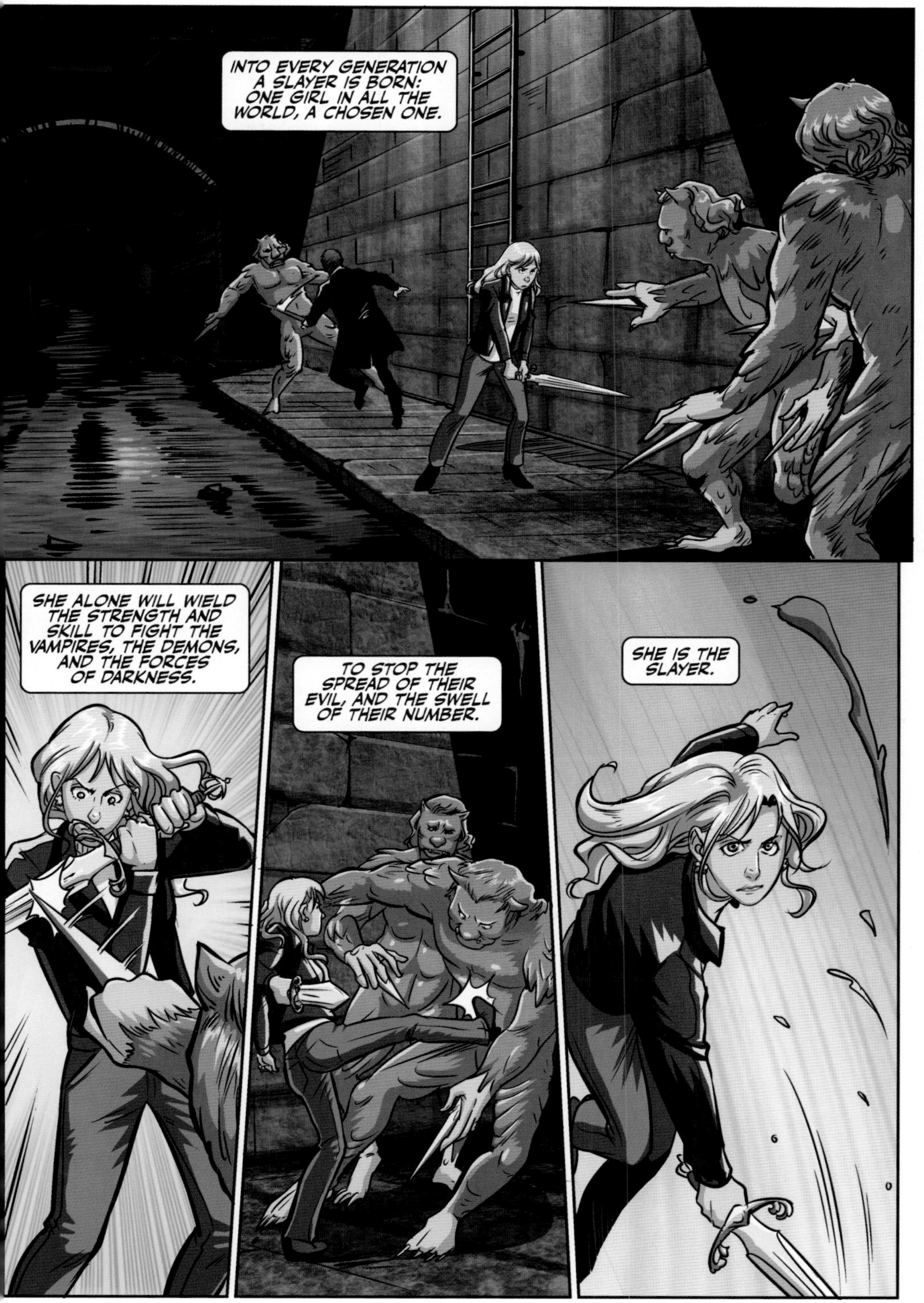
INTO EVERY GENERATION A SLAYER IS BORN: ONE GIRL IN ALL THE WORLD, A CHOSEN ONE.
SHE ALONE WILL WIELD THE STRENGTH AND SKILL TO FIGHT THE VAMPIRES, THE DEMONS, AND THE FORCES OF DARKNESS.
TO STOP THE SPREAD OF THEIR EVIL, AND THE SWELL OF THEIR NUMBER.
SHE IS THE SLAYER.

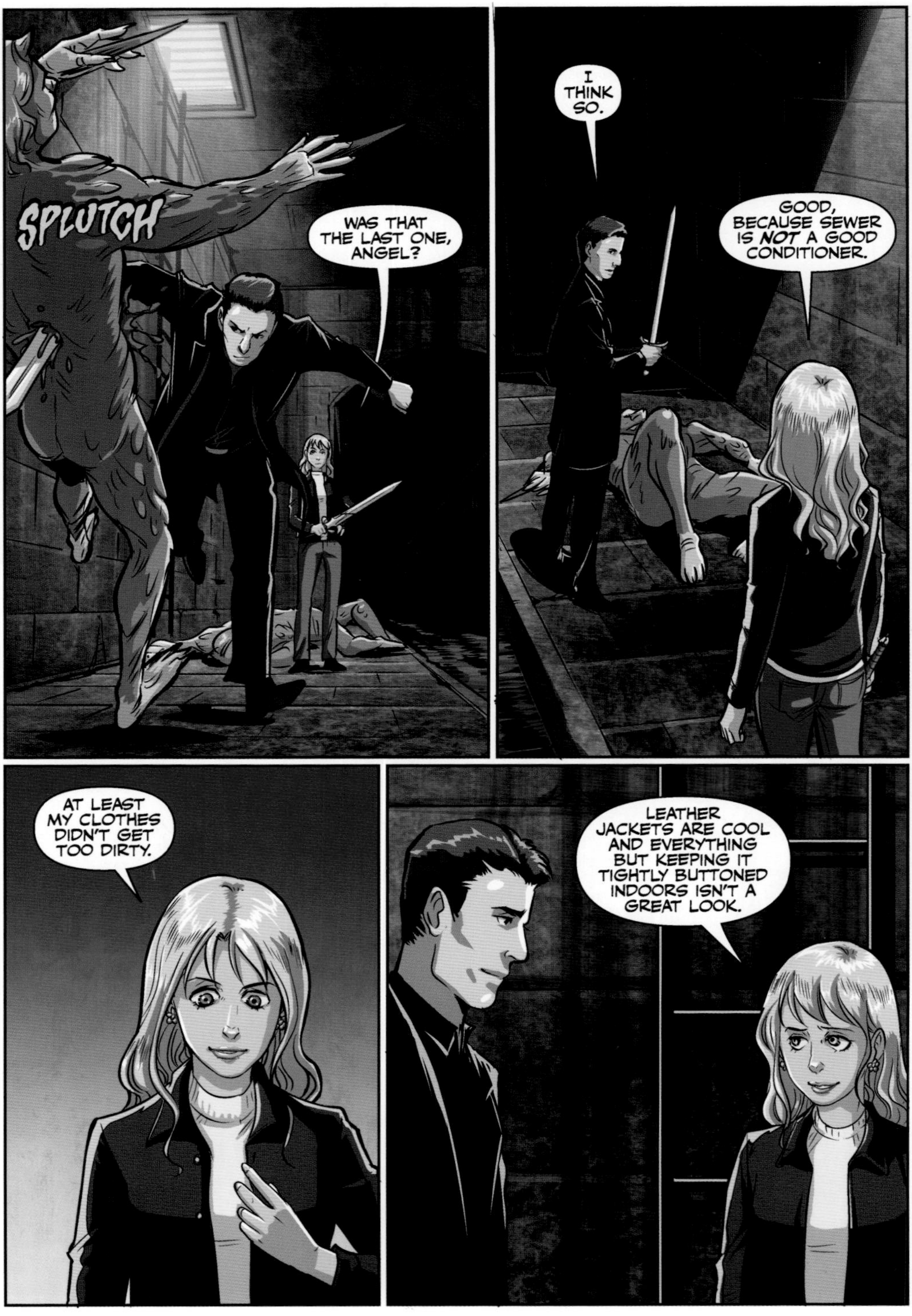
SPLUTCH
WAS THAT THE LAST ONE, ANGEL?
I THINK SO.
GOOD, BECAUSE SEWER IS *NOT* A GOOD CONDITIONER.
AT LEAST MY CLOTHES DIDN'T GET TOO DIRTY.
LEATHER JACKETS ARE COOL AND EVERYTHING BUT KEEPING IT TIGHTLY BUTTONED INDOORS ISN'T A GREAT LOOK.

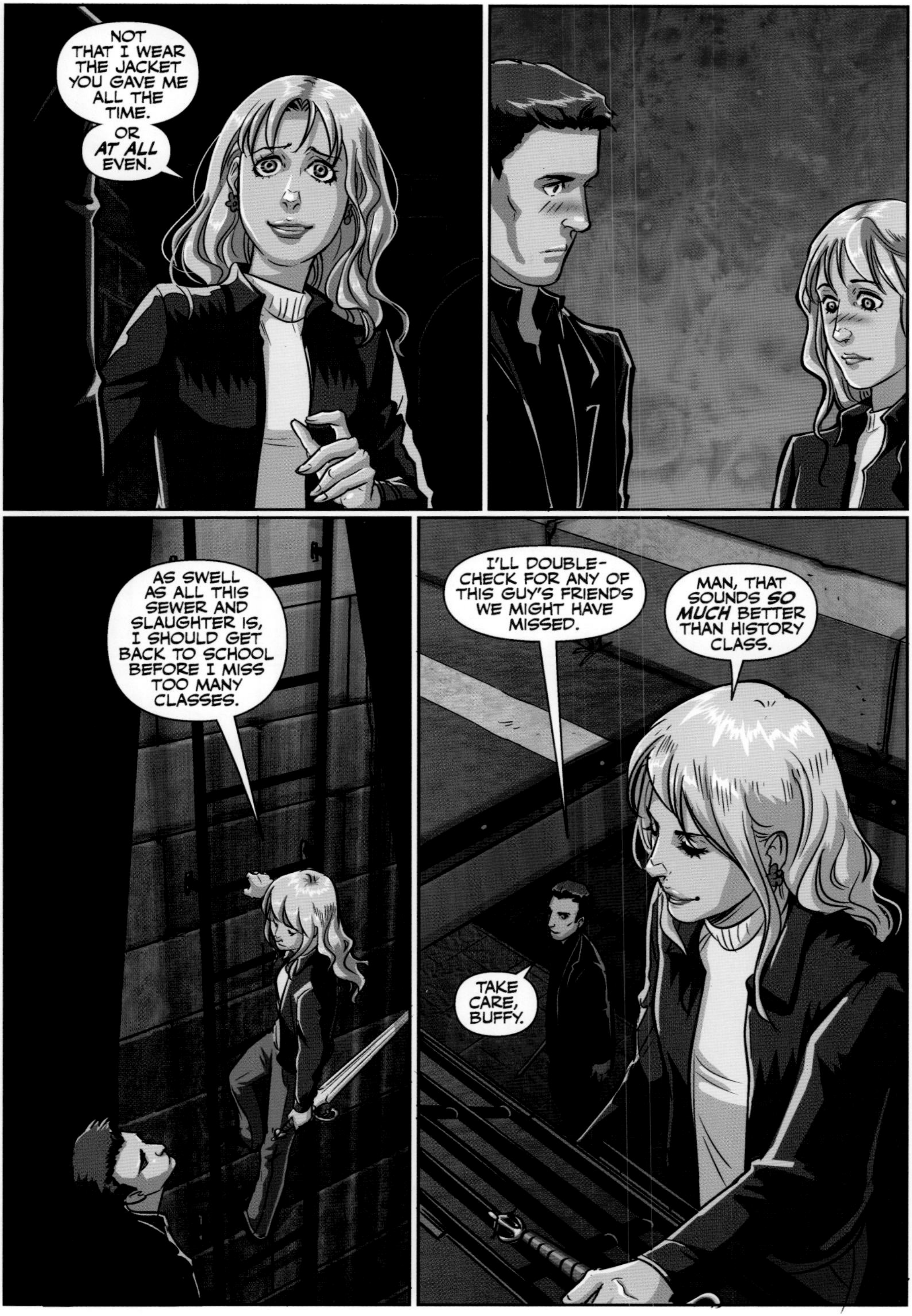
NOT THAT I WEAR THE JACKET YOU GAVE ME ALL THE TIME.
OR AT ALL EVEN.
AS SWELL AS ALL THIS SEWER AND SLAUGHTER IS, I SHOULD GET BACK TO SCHOOL BEFORE I MISS TOO MANY CLASSES.
I'LL DOUBLE-CHECK FOR ANY OF THIS GUY'S FRIENDS WE MIGHT HAVE MISSED.
MAN, THAT SOUNDS SO MUCH BETTER THAN HISTORY CLASS.
TAKE CARE, BUFFY.

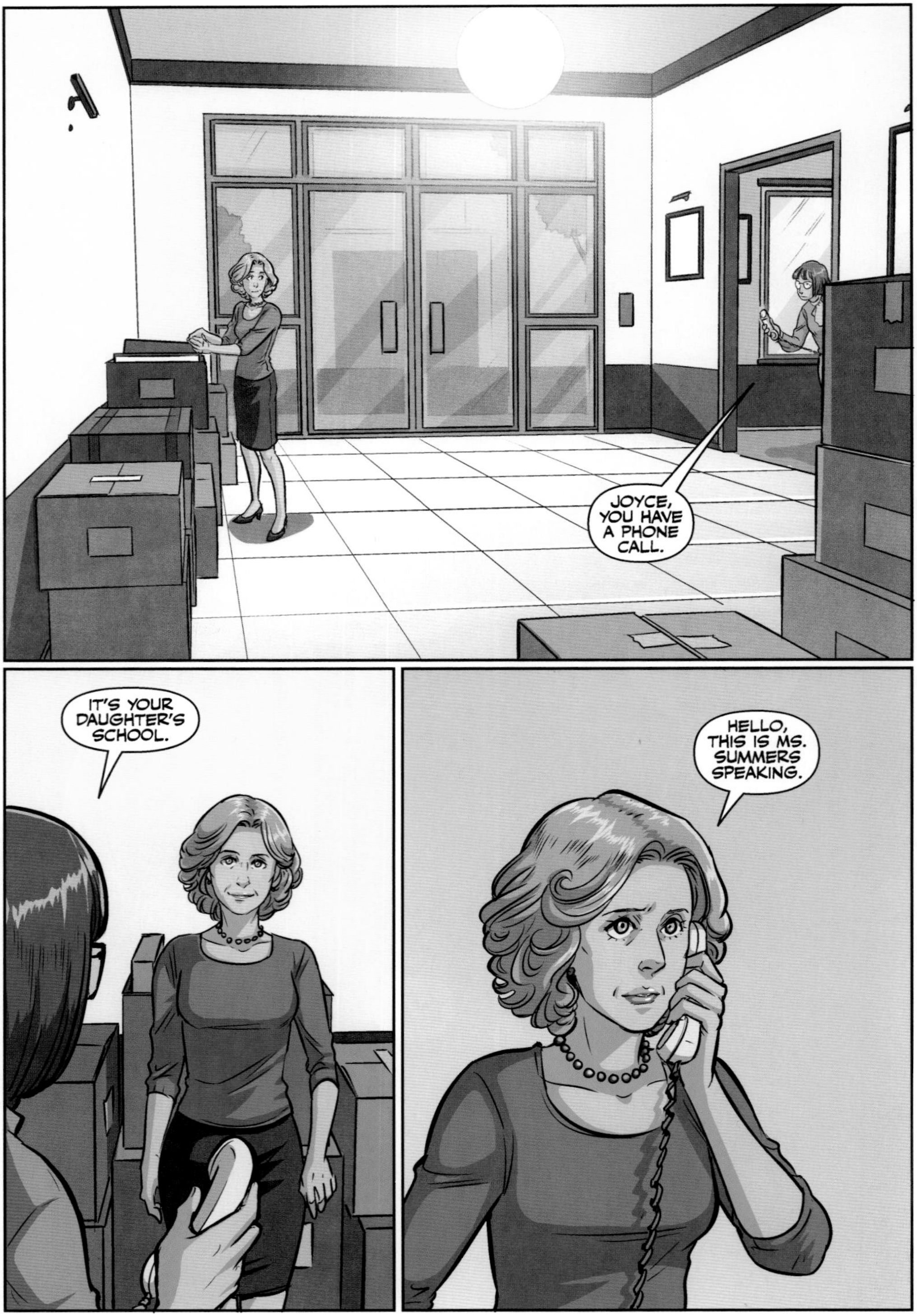
JOYCE, YOU HAVE A PHONE CALL.
IT'S YOUR DAUGHTER'S SCHOOL.
HELLO, THIS IS MS. SUMMERS SPEAKING.

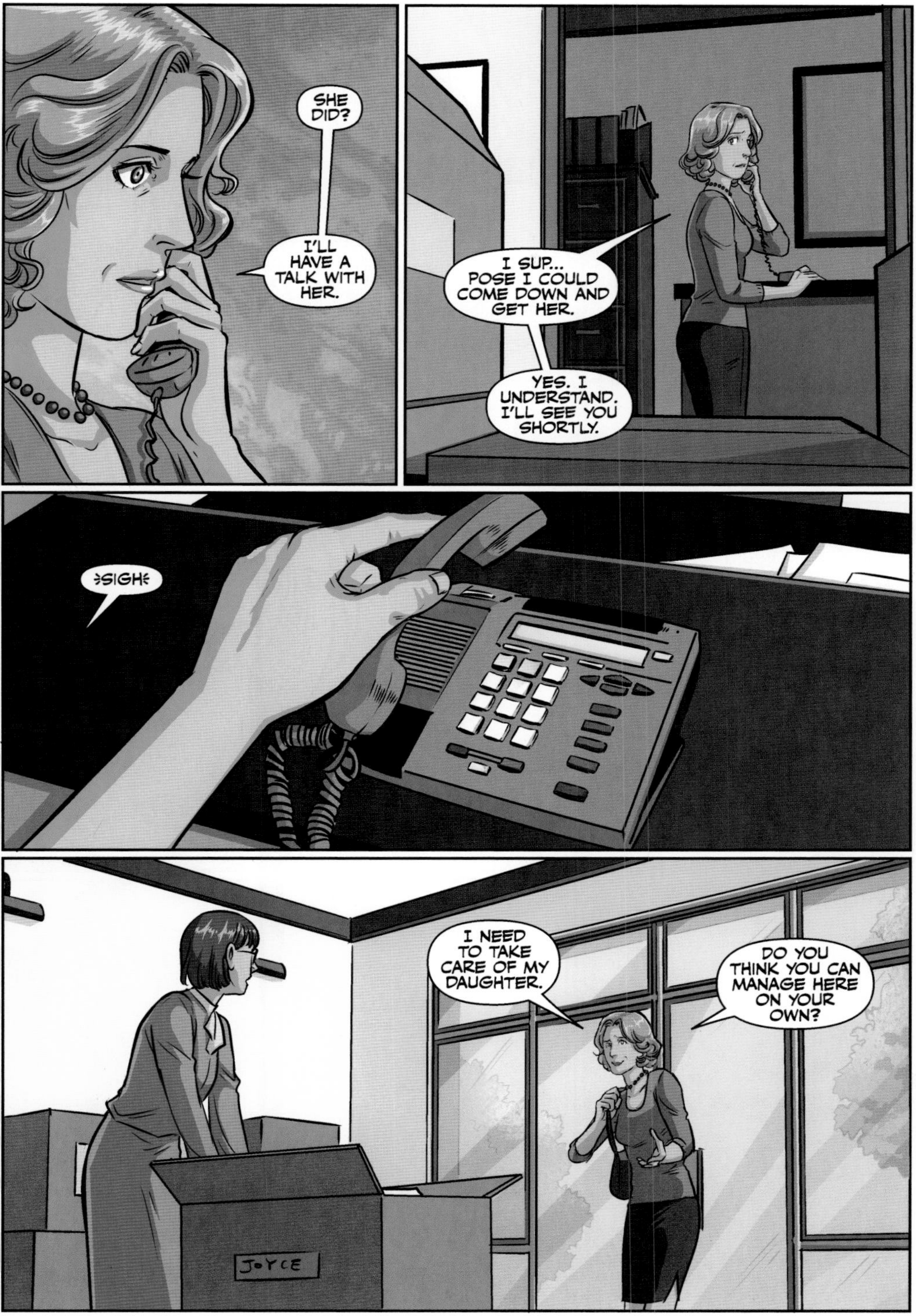
SHE DID?
I'LL HAVE A TALK WITH HER.
I SUP... POSE I COULD COME DOWN AND GET HER.
YES. I UNDERSTAND. I'LL SEE YOU SHORTLY.
SIGH
I NEED TO TAKE CARE OF MY DAUGHTER.
DO YOU THINK YOU CAN MANAGE HERE ON YOUR OWN?
JOYCE

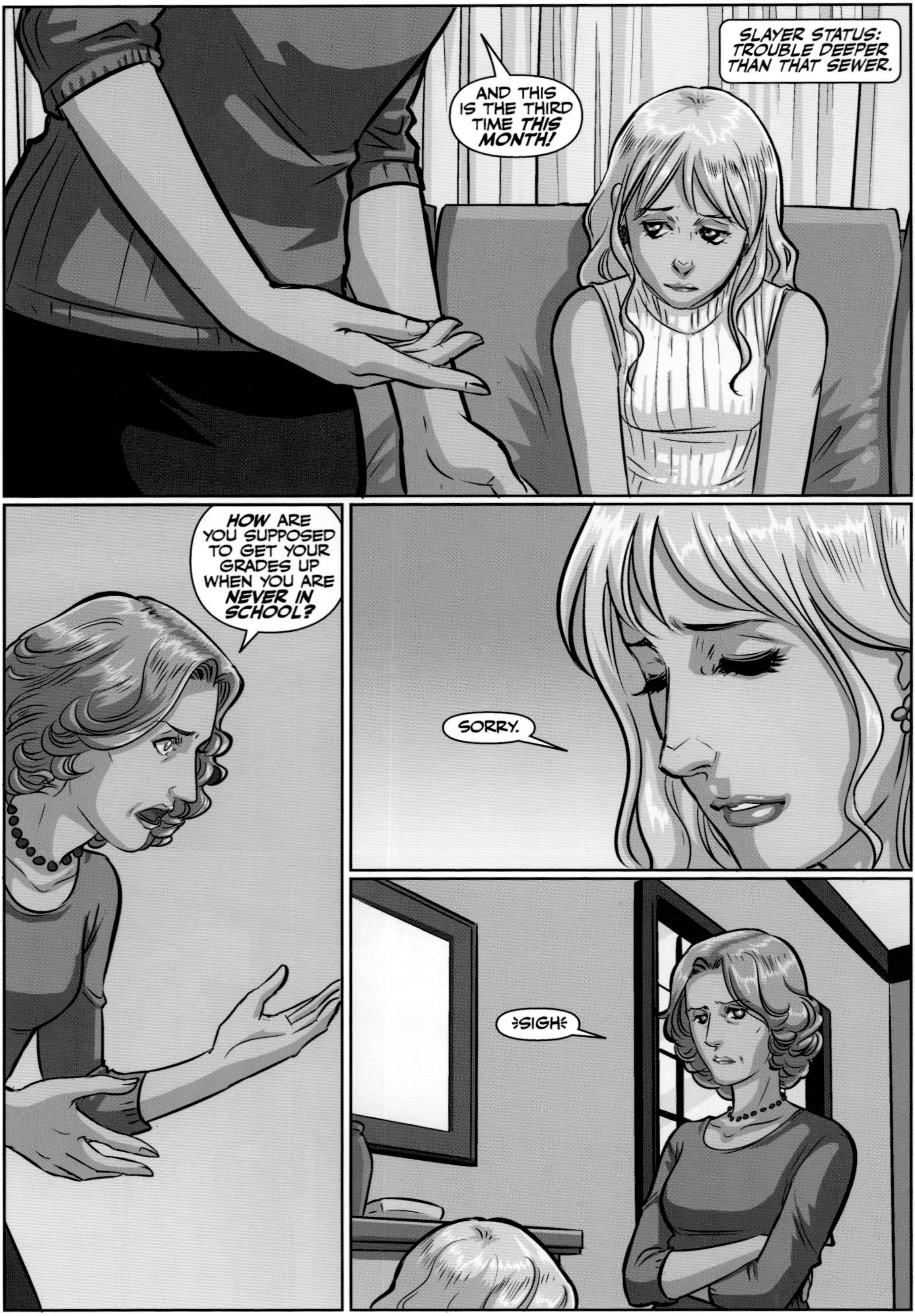
SLAYER STATUS: TROUBLE DEEPER THAN THAT SEWER.
AND THIS IS THE THIRD TIME *THIS MONTH!*
HOW ARE YOU SUPPOSED TO GET YOUR GRADES UP WHEN YOU ARE *NEVER IN SCHOOL?*
SORRY.
SIGH

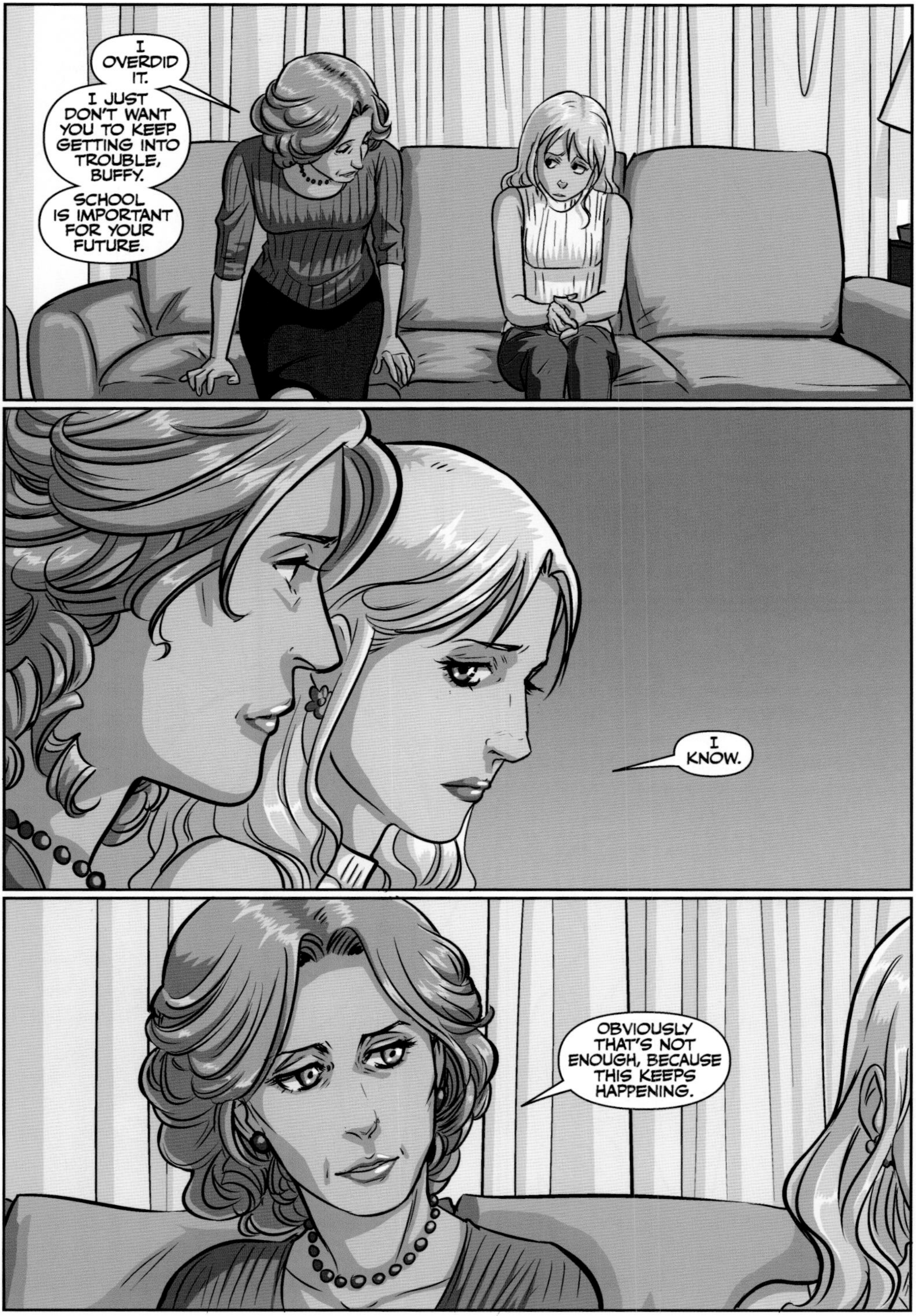
I OVERDID IT.
I JUST DON'T WANT YOU TO KEEP GETTING INTO TROUBLE, BUFFY.
SCHOOL IS IMPORTANT FOR YOUR FUTURE.
I KNOW.
OBVIOUSLY THAT'S NOT ENOUGH, BECAUSE THIS KEEPS HAPPENING.

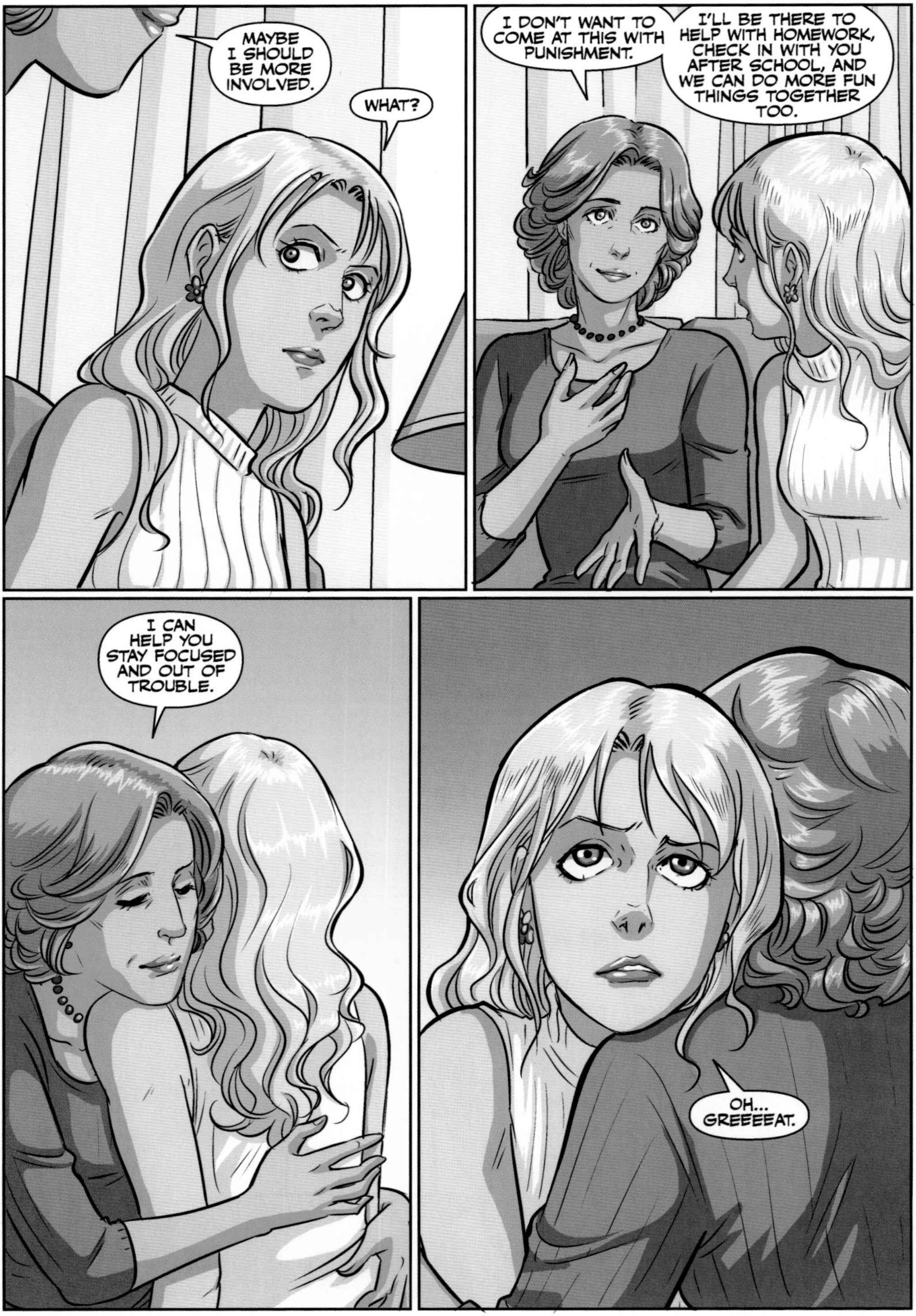
MAYBE I SHOULD BE MORE INVOLVED.
WHAT?
I DON'T WANT TO COME AT THIS WITH PUNISHMENT.
I'LL BE THERE TO HELP WITH HOMEWORK, CHECK IN WITH YOU AFTER SCHOOL, AND WE CAN DO MORE FUN THINGS TOGETHER TOO.
I CAN HELP YOU STAY FOCUSED AND OUT OF TROUBLE.
OH... GREEEEAT.

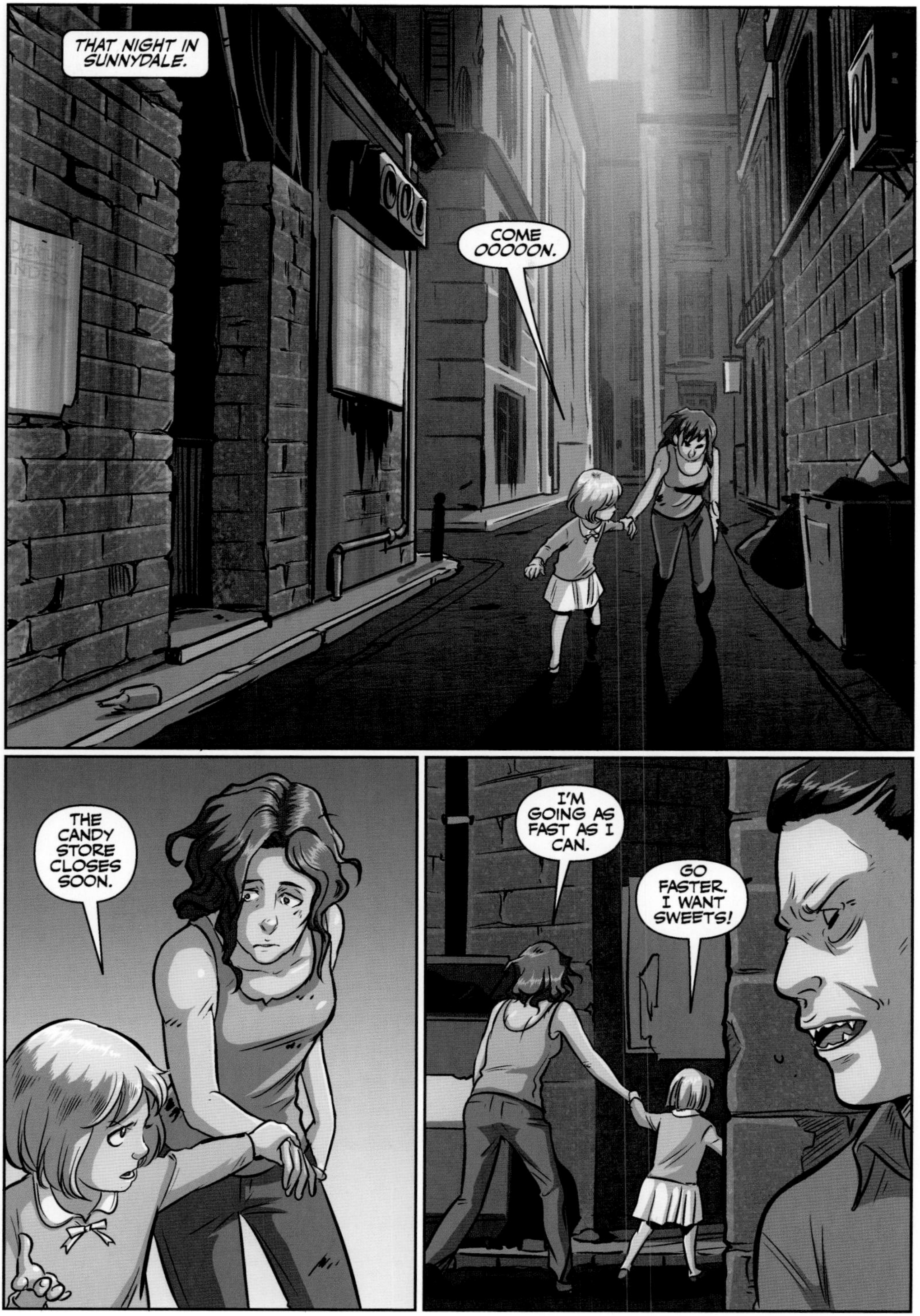
THAT NIGHT IN SUNNYDALE.
COME OOOOON.
THE CANDY STORE CLOSES SOON.
I'M GOING AS FAST AS I CAN.
GO FASTER. I WANT SWEETS!

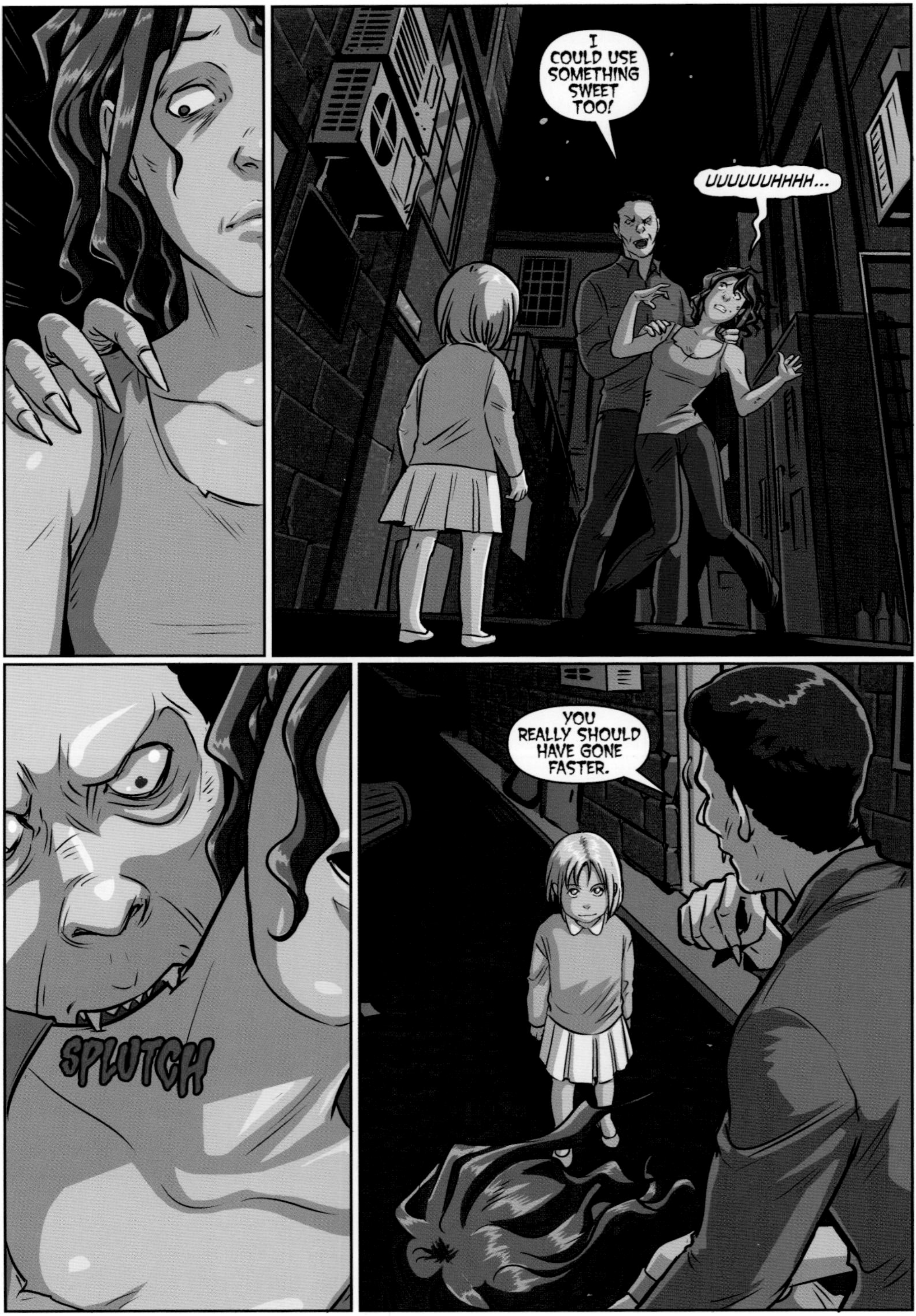

I COULD USE SOMETHING SWEET TOO!
UUUUUUHHHH...
SPLUTCH
YOU REALLY SHOULD HAVE GONE FASTER.

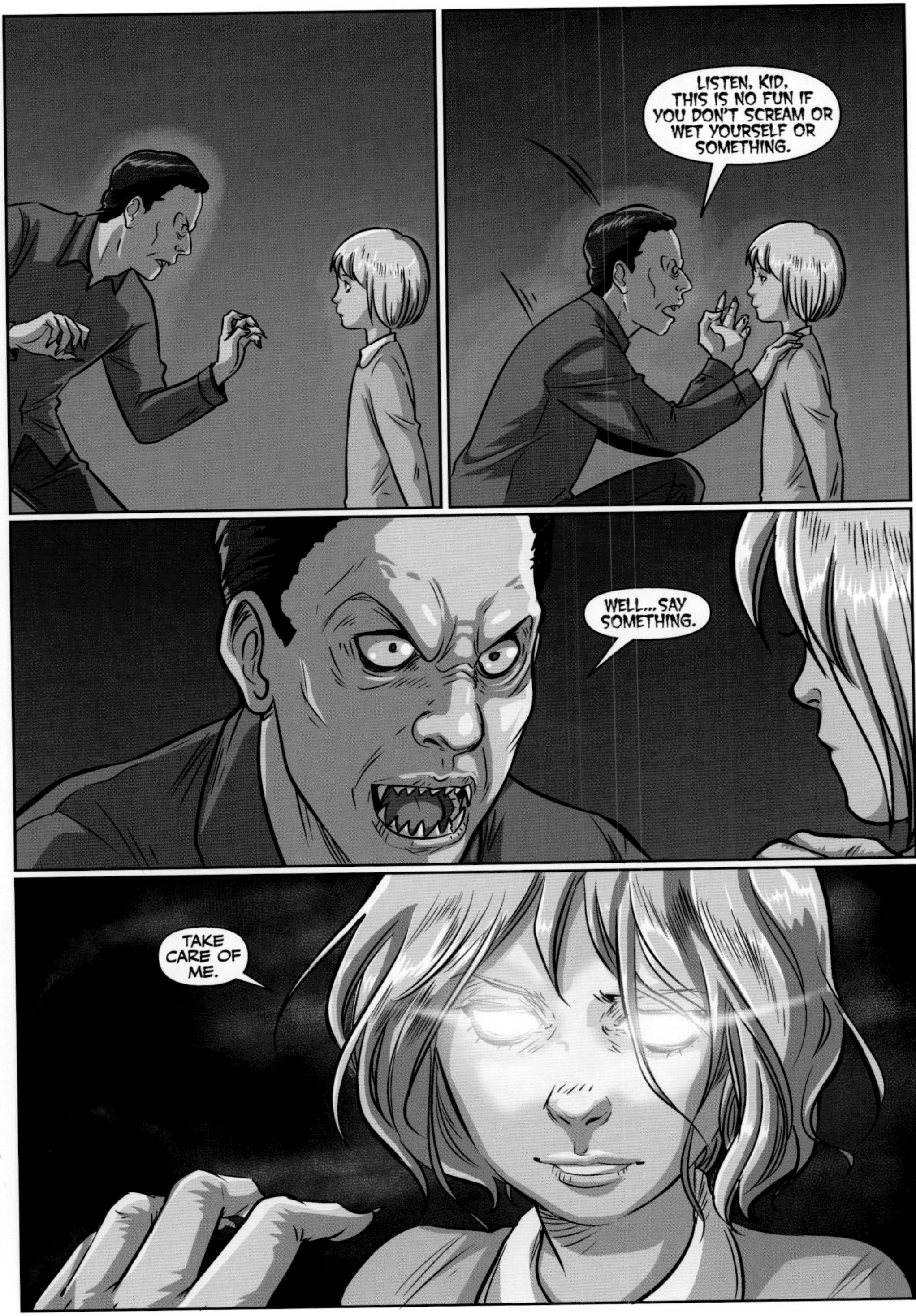
LISTEN, KID, THIS IS NO FUN IF YOU DON'T SCREAM OR WET YOURSELF OR SOMETHING.
WELL... SAY SOMETHING.
TAKE CARE OF ME.

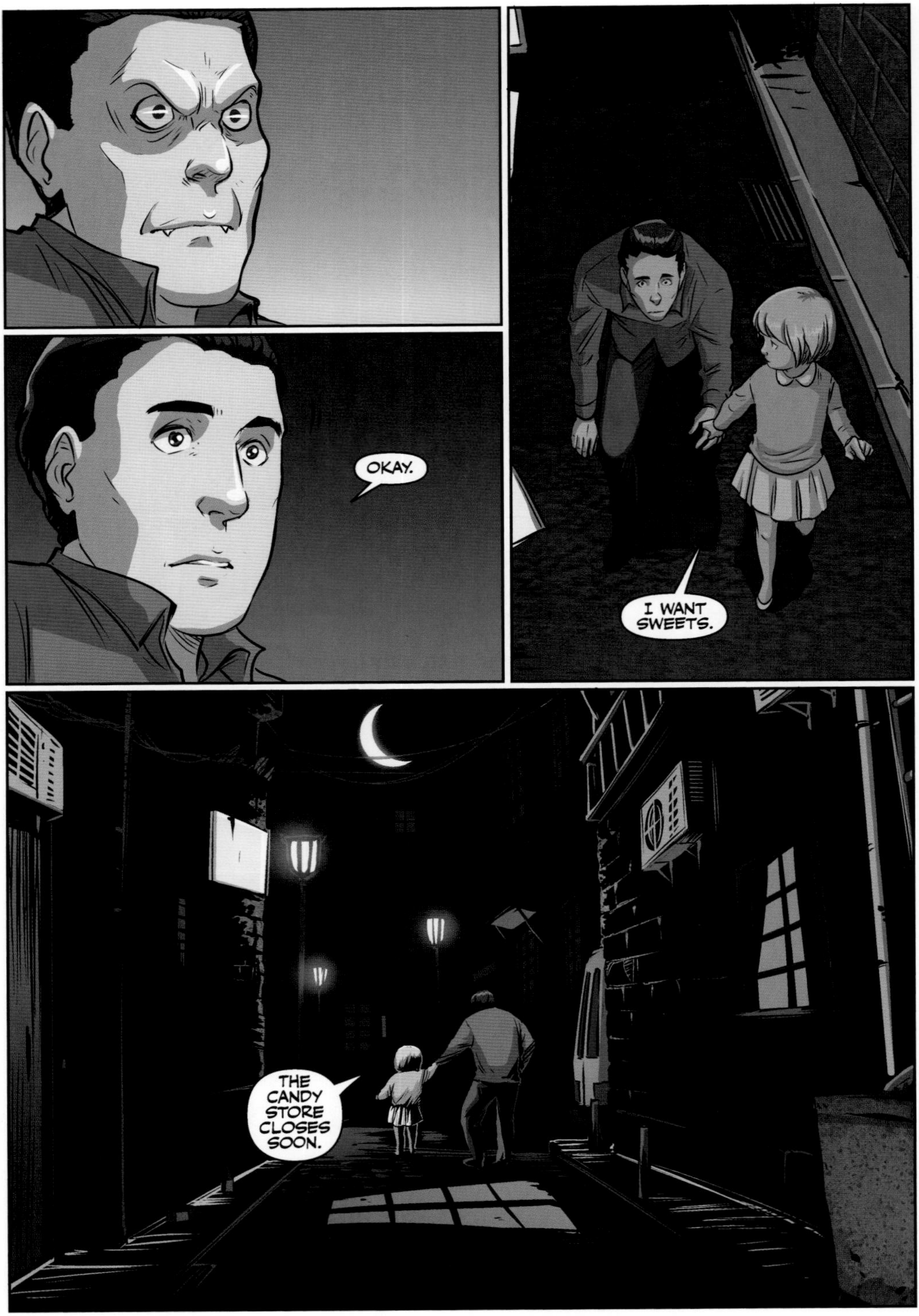
OKAY.
I WANT SWEETS.
THE CANDY STORE CLOSES SOON.

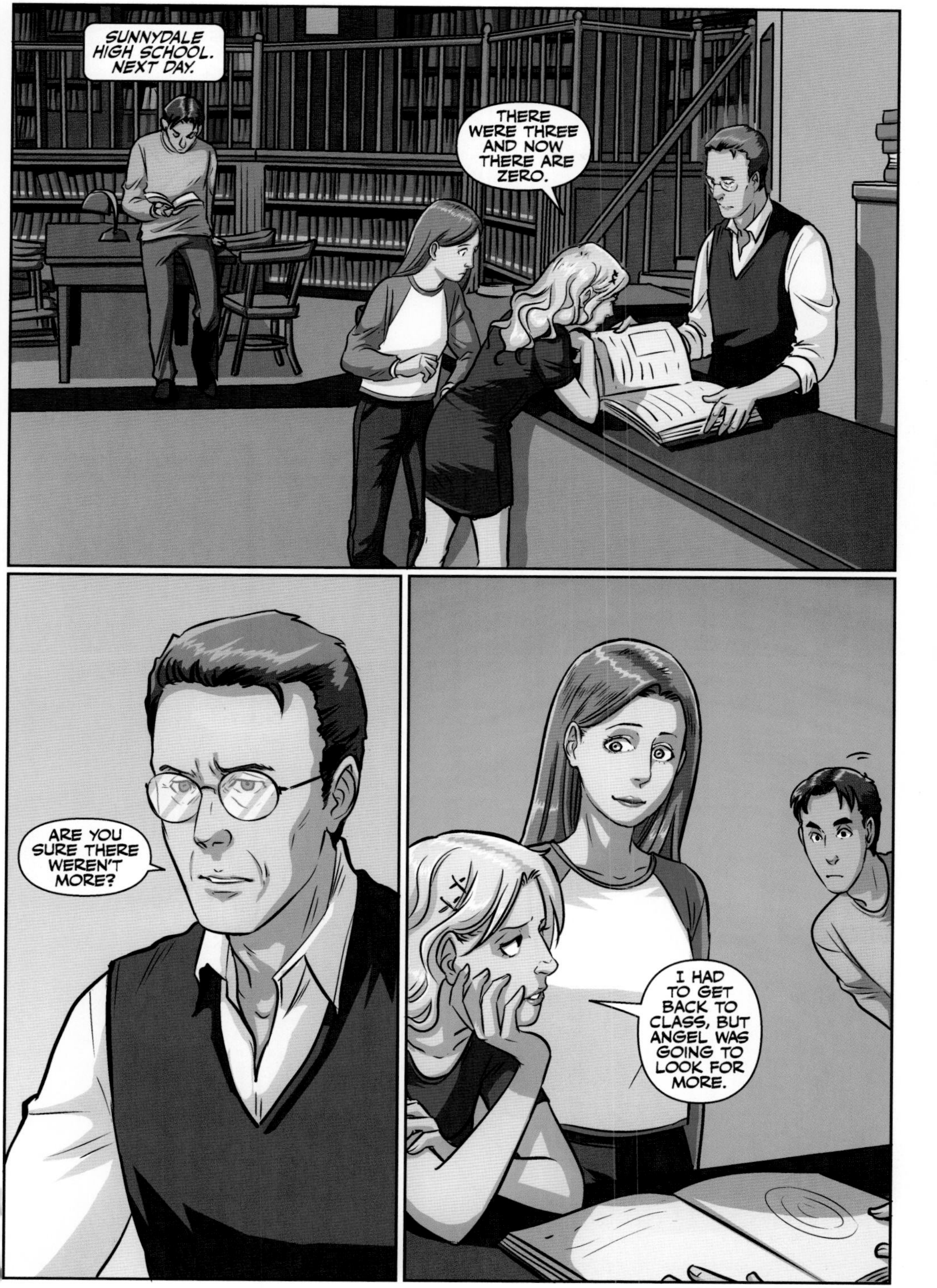
SUNNYDALE HIGH SCHOOL. NEXT DAY.
THERE WERE THREE AND NOW THERE ARE ZERO.
ARE YOU SURE THERE WEREN'T MORE?
I HAD TO GET BACK TO CLASS, BUT ANGEL WAS GOING TO LOOK FOR MORE.

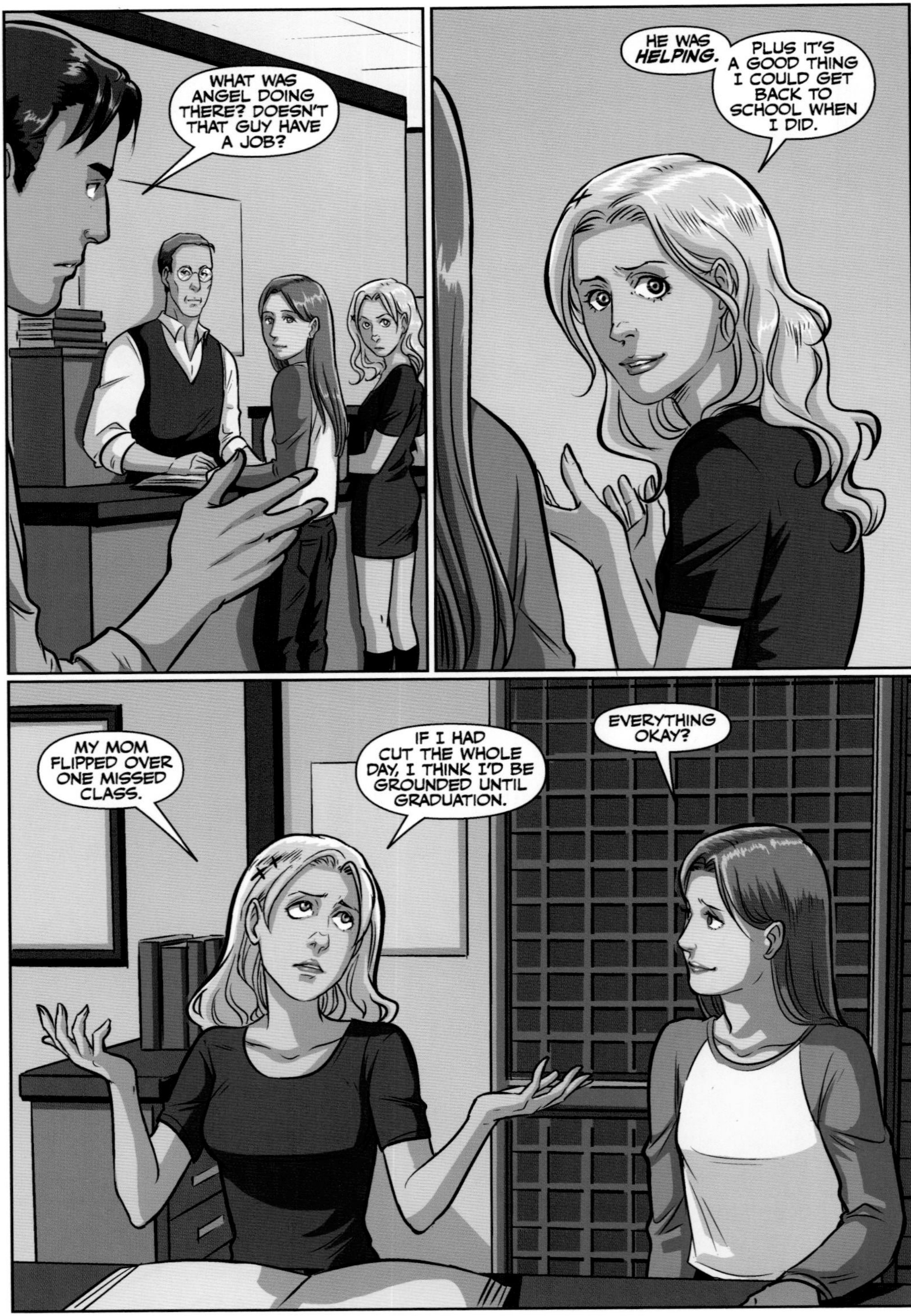
WHAT WAS ANGEL DOING THERE? DOESN'T THAT GUY HAVE A JOB?
HE WAS *HELPING.*
PLUS IT'S A GOOD THING I COULD GET BACK TO SCHOOL WHEN I DID.
MY MOM FLIPPED OVER ONE MISSED CLASS.
IF I HAD CUT THE WHOLE DAY, I THINK I'D BE GROUNDED UNTIL GRADUATION.
EVERYTHING OKAY?

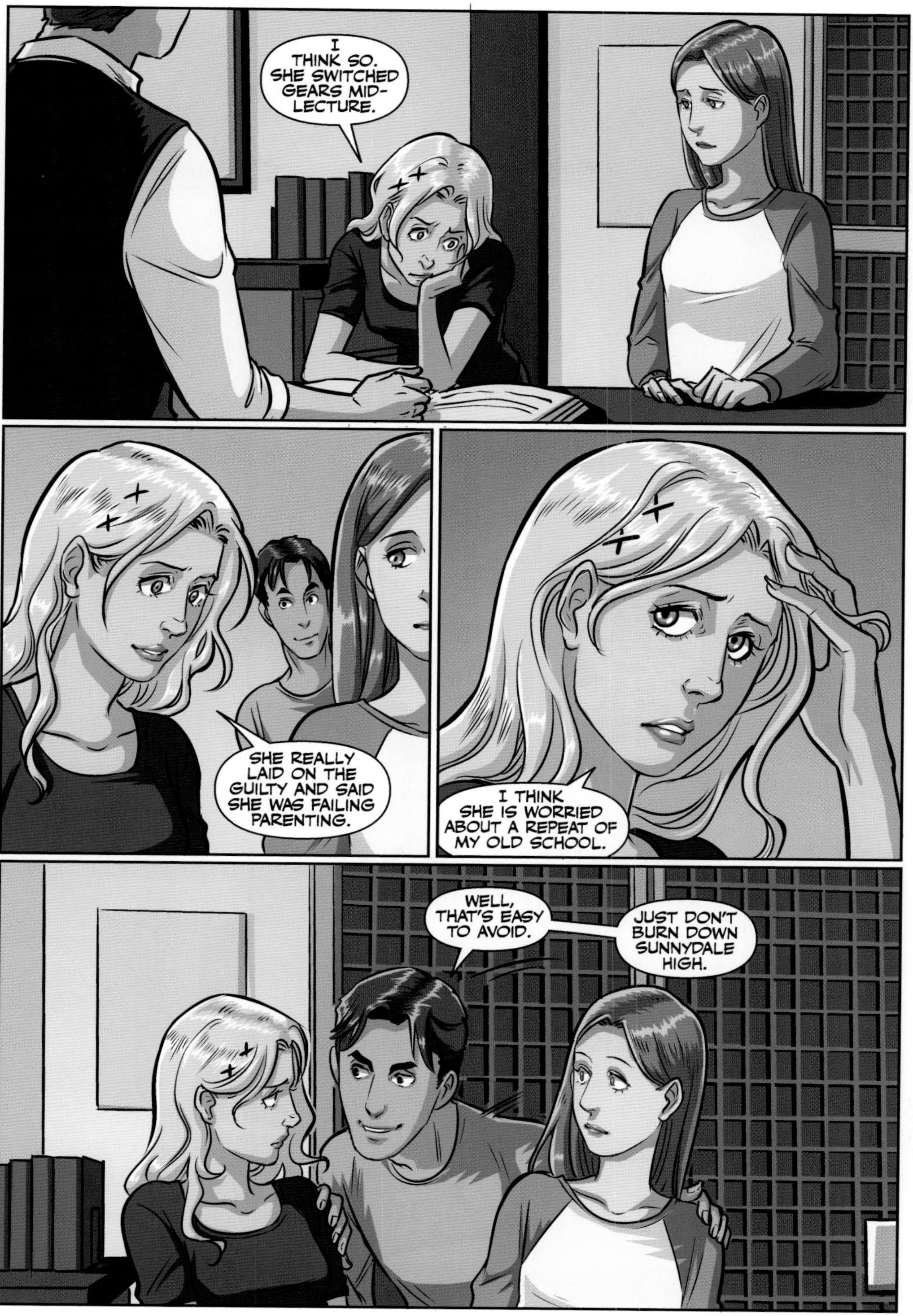
I THINK SO. SHE SWITCHED GEARS MID-LECTURE.
SHE REALLY LAID ON THE GUILTY AND SAID SHE WAS FAILING PARENTING.
I THINK SHE IS WORRIED ABOUT A REPEAT OF MY OLD SCHOOL.
WELL, THAT'S EASY TO AVOID.
JUST DON'T BURN DOWN SUNNYDALE HIGH.

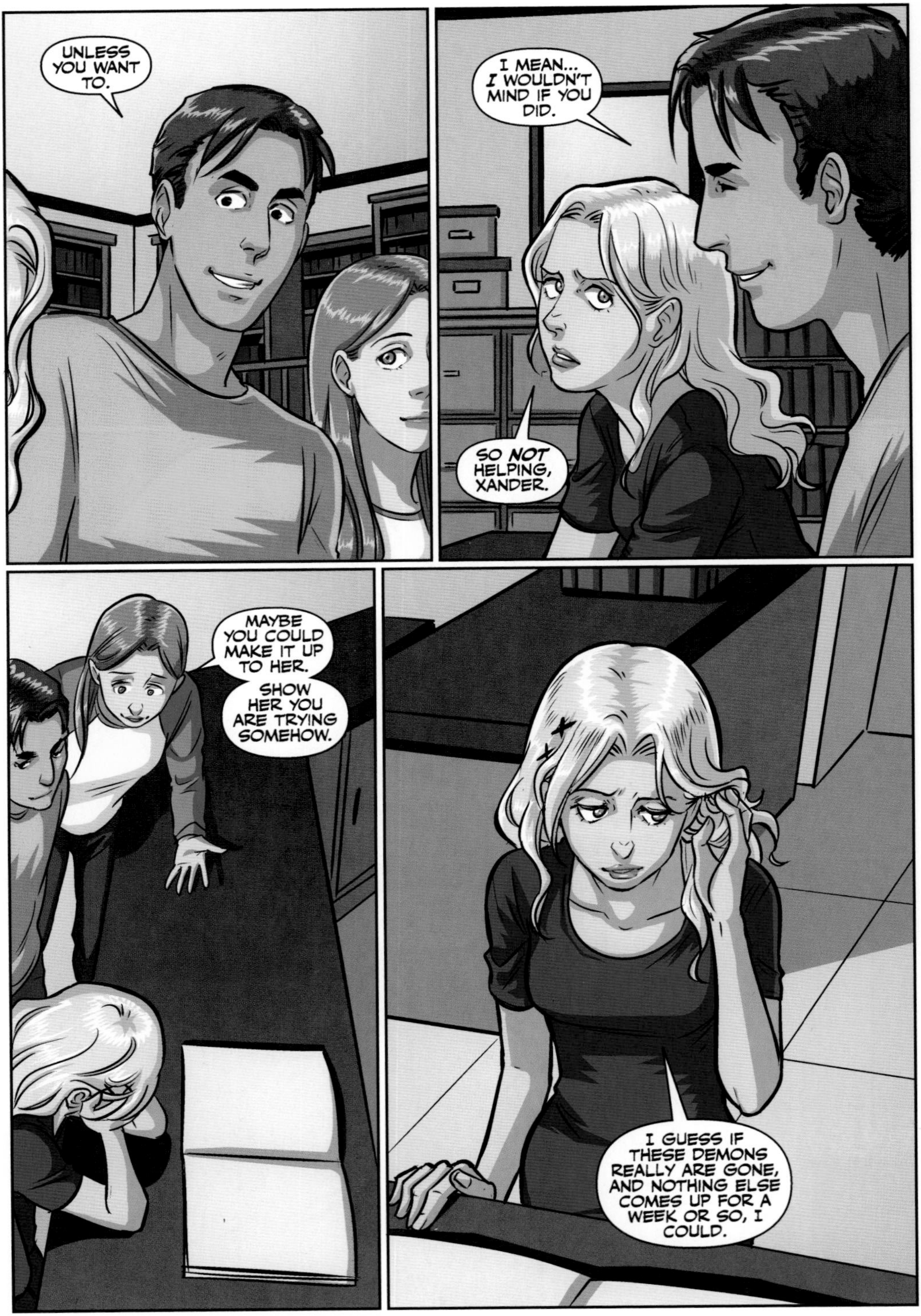
UNLESS YOU WANT TO.
I MEAN... I WOULDN'T MIND IF YOU DID.
SO NOT HELPING, XANDER.
MAYBE YOU COULD MAKE IT UP TO HER.
SHOW HER YOU ARE TRYING SOMEHOW.
I GUESS IF THESE DEMONS REALLY ARE GONE, AND NOTHING ELSE COMES UP FOR A WEEK OR SO, I COULD.

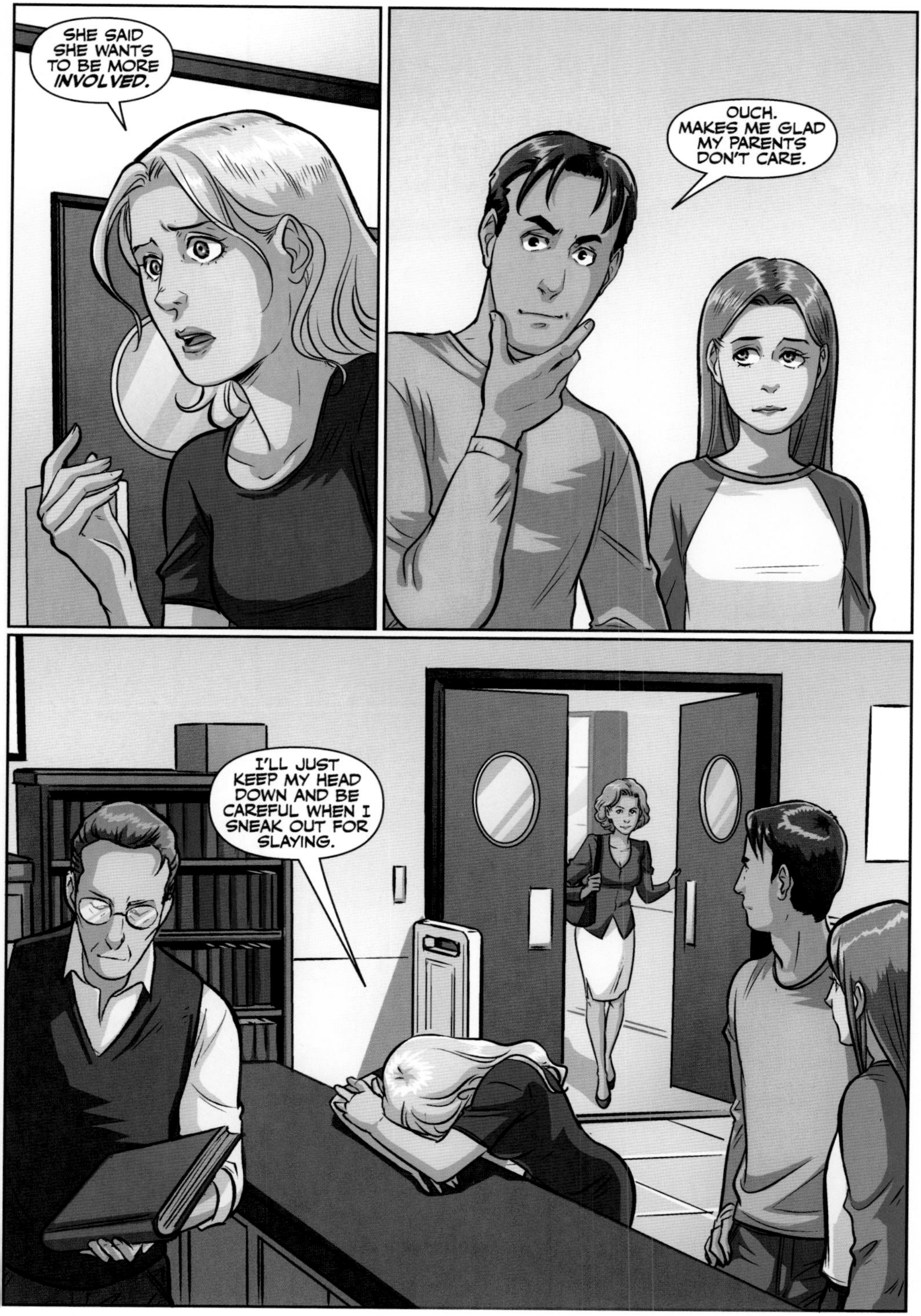
SHE SAID SHE WANTS TO BE MORE *INVOLVED.*
OUCH. MAKES ME GLAD MY PARENTS DON'T CARE.
I'LL JUST KEEP MY HEAD DOWN AND BE CAREFUL WHEN I SNEAK OUT FOR SLAYING.

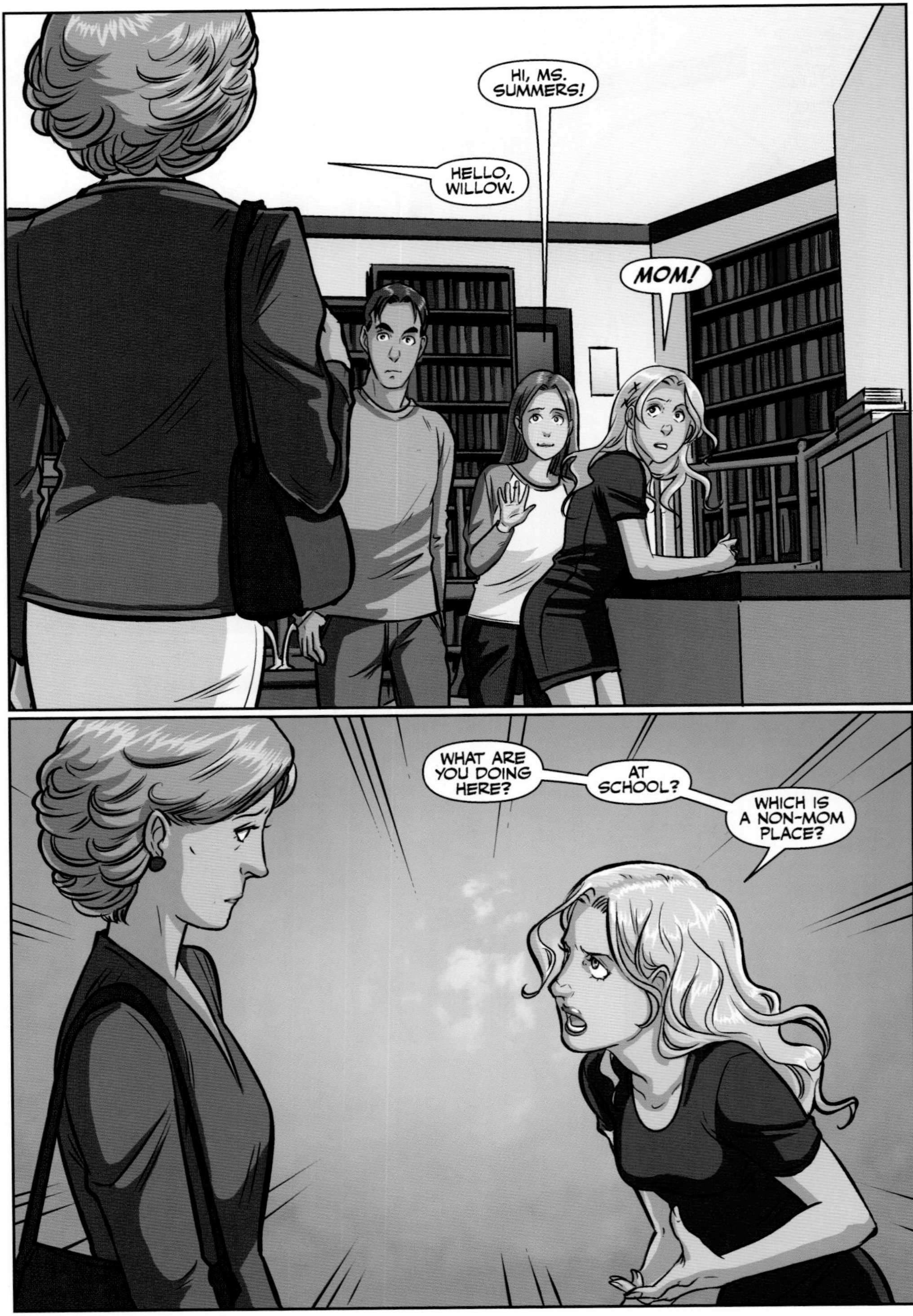
HELLO, WILLOW.
HI, MS. SUMMERS!
MOM!
WHAT ARE YOU DOING HERE?
AT SCHOOL?
WHICH IS A NON-MOM PLACE?

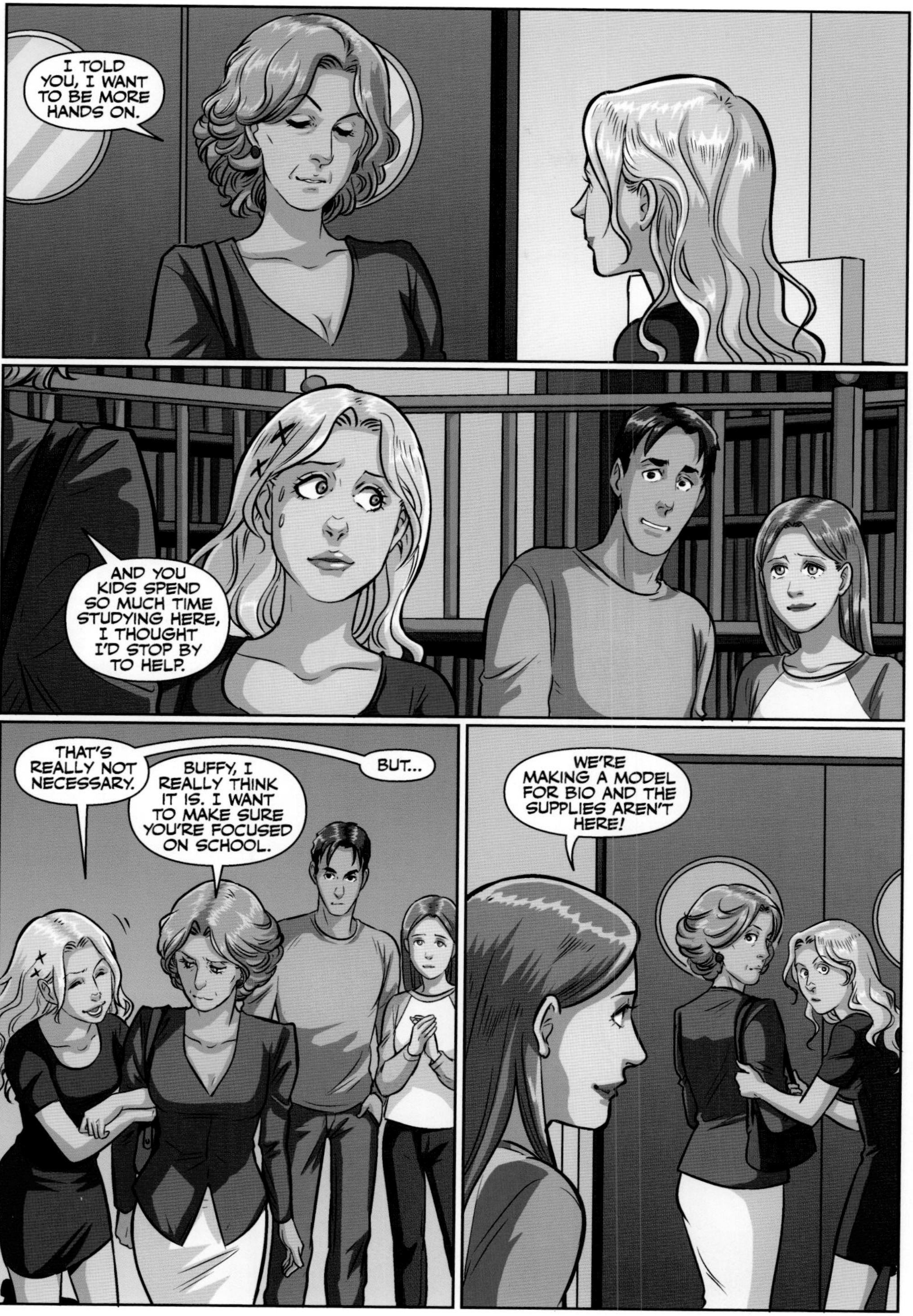
I TOLD YOU, I WANT TO BE MORE HANDS ON.
AND YOU KIDS SPEND SO MUCH TIME STUDYING HERE, I THOUGHT I'D STOP BY TO HELP.
THAT'S REALLY NOT NECESSARY.
BUFFY, I REALLY THINK IT IS. I WANT TO MAKE SURE YOU'RE FOCUSED ON SCHOOL.
BUT...
WE'RE MAKING A MODEL FOR BIO AND THE SUPPLIES AREN'T HERE!

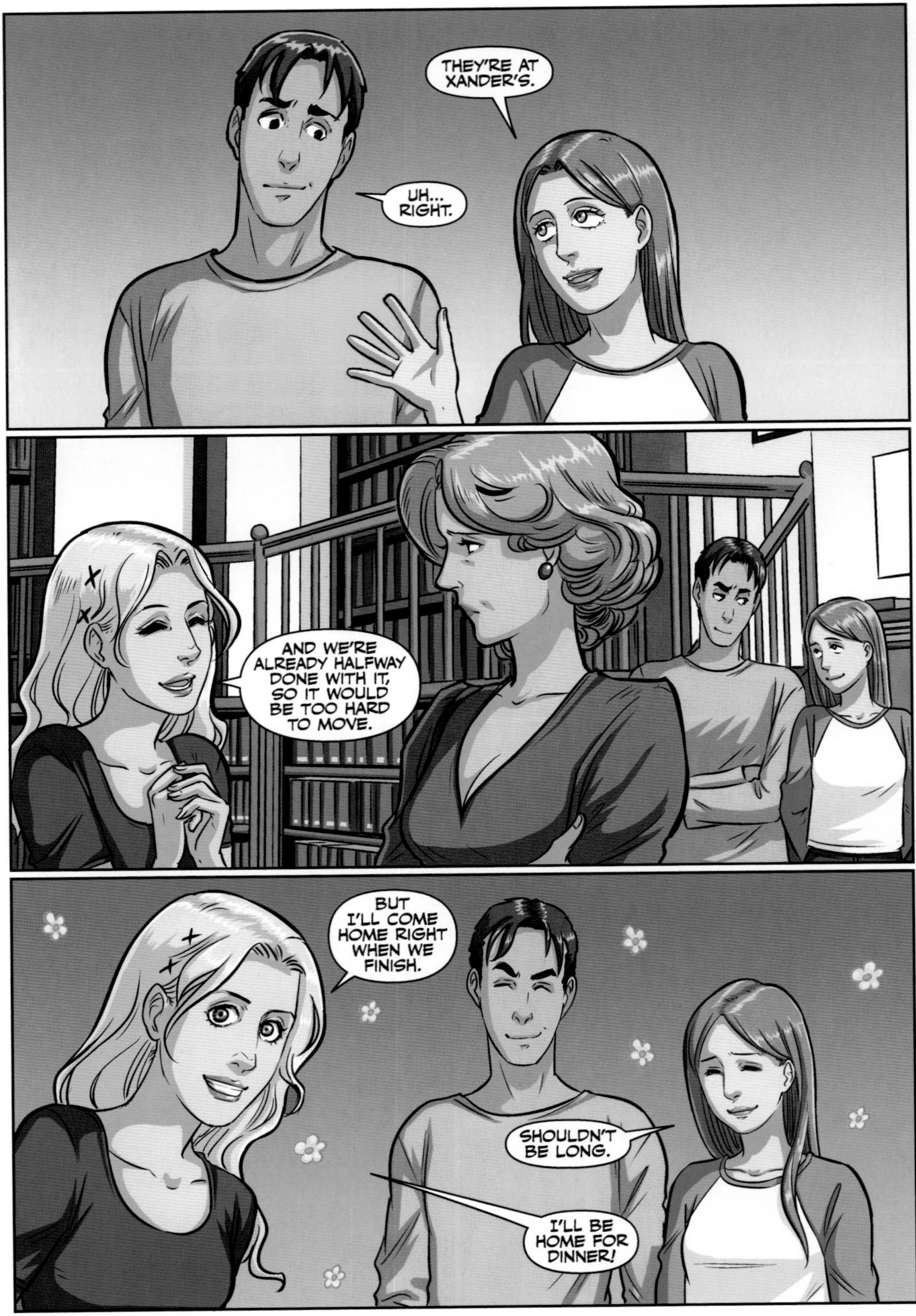
THEY'RE AT XANDER'S.
UH... RIGHT.
AND WE'RE ALREADY HALFWAY DONE WITH IT, SO IT WOULD BE TOO HARD TO MOVE.
BUT I'LL COME HOME RIGHT WHEN WE FINISH.
SHOULDN'T BE LONG.
I'LL BE HOME FOR DINNER!

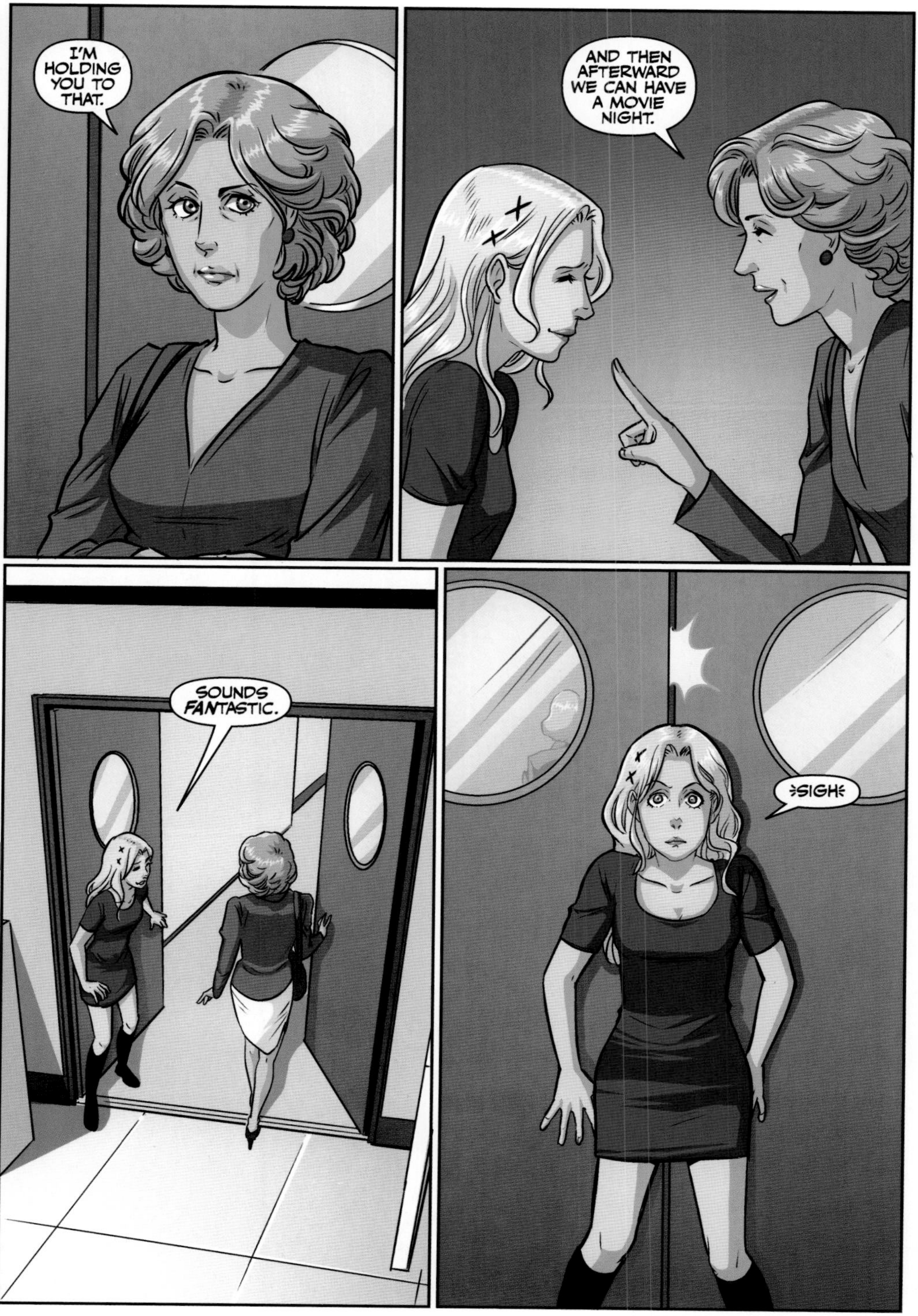
I'M HOLDING YOU TO THAT.
AND THEN AFTERWARD WE CAN HAVE A MOVIE NIGHT.
SOUNDS FANTASTIC.
SIGH

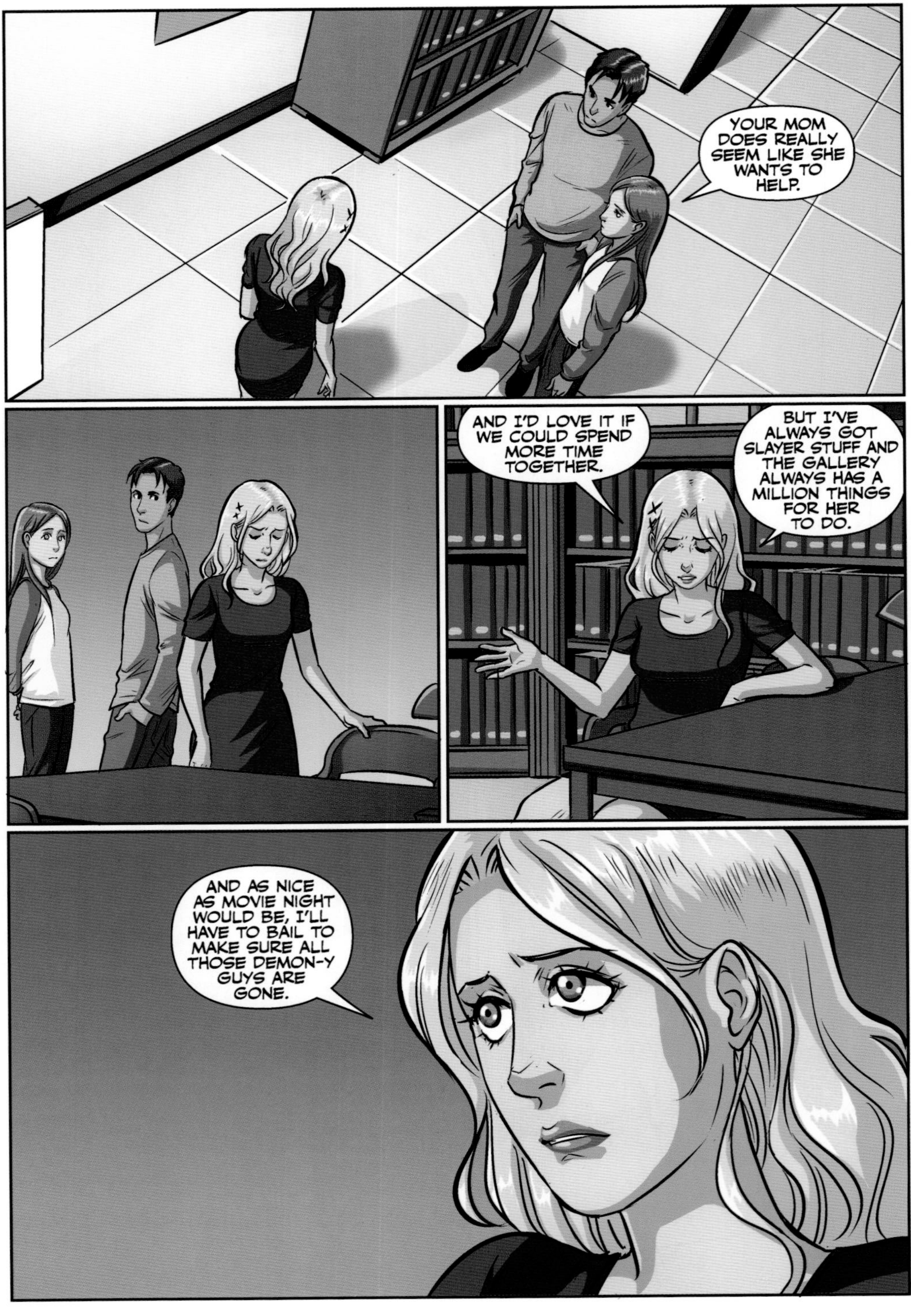
YOUR MOM DOES REALLY SEEM LIKE SHE WANTS TO HELP.
AND I'D LOVE IT IF WE COULD SPEND MORE TIME TOGETHER.
BUT I'VE ALWAYS GOT SLAYER STUFF AND THE GALLERY ALWAYS HAS A MILLION THINGS FOR HER TO DO.
AND AS NICE AS MOVIE NIGHT WOULD BE, I'LL HAVE TO BAIL TO MAKE SURE ALL THOSE DEMON-Y GUYS ARE GONE.

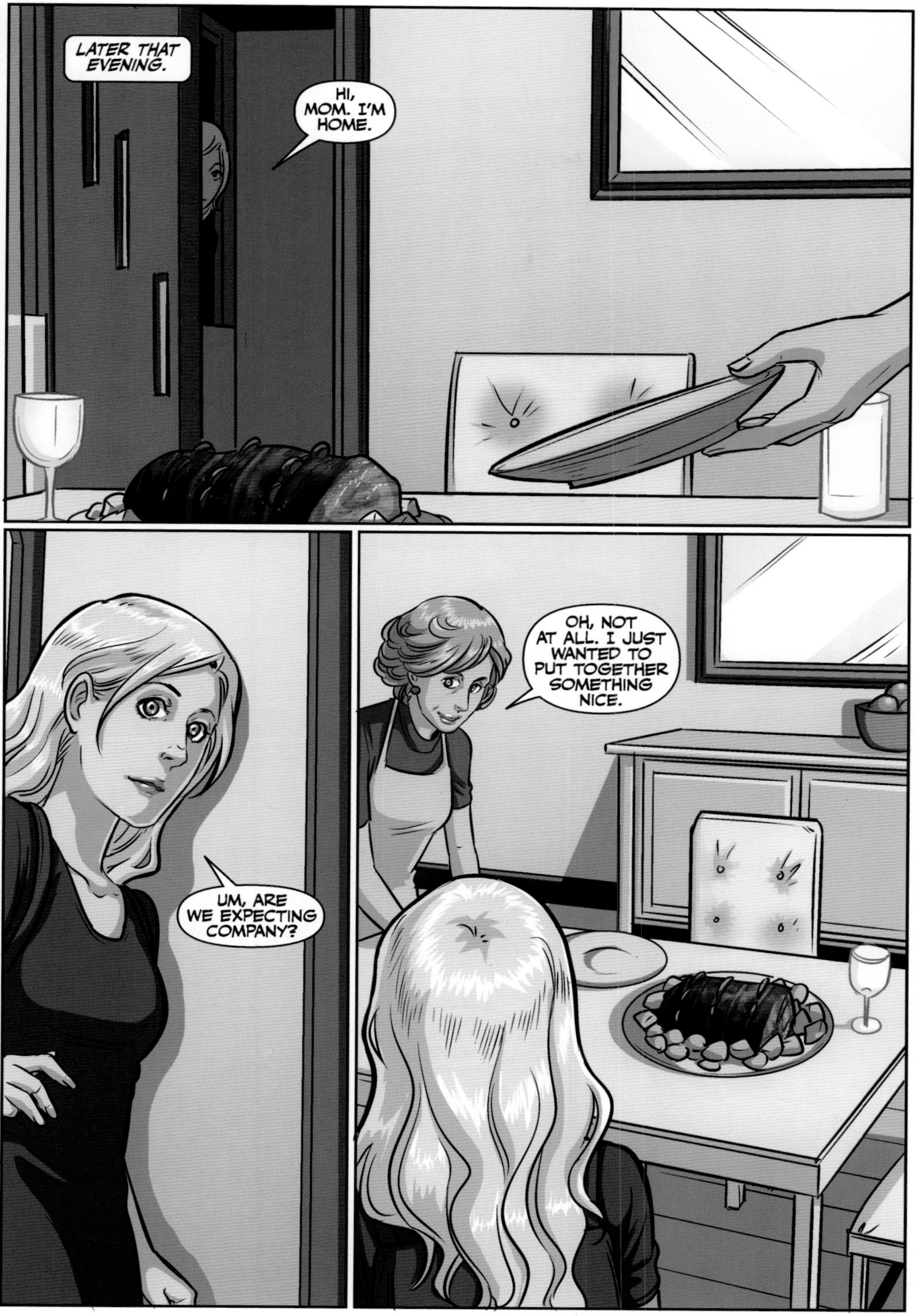
LATER THAT EVENING.
HI, MOM. I'M HOME.
UM, ARE WE EXPECTING COMPANY?
OH, NOT AT ALL. I JUST WANTED TO PUT TOGETHER SOMETHING NICE.

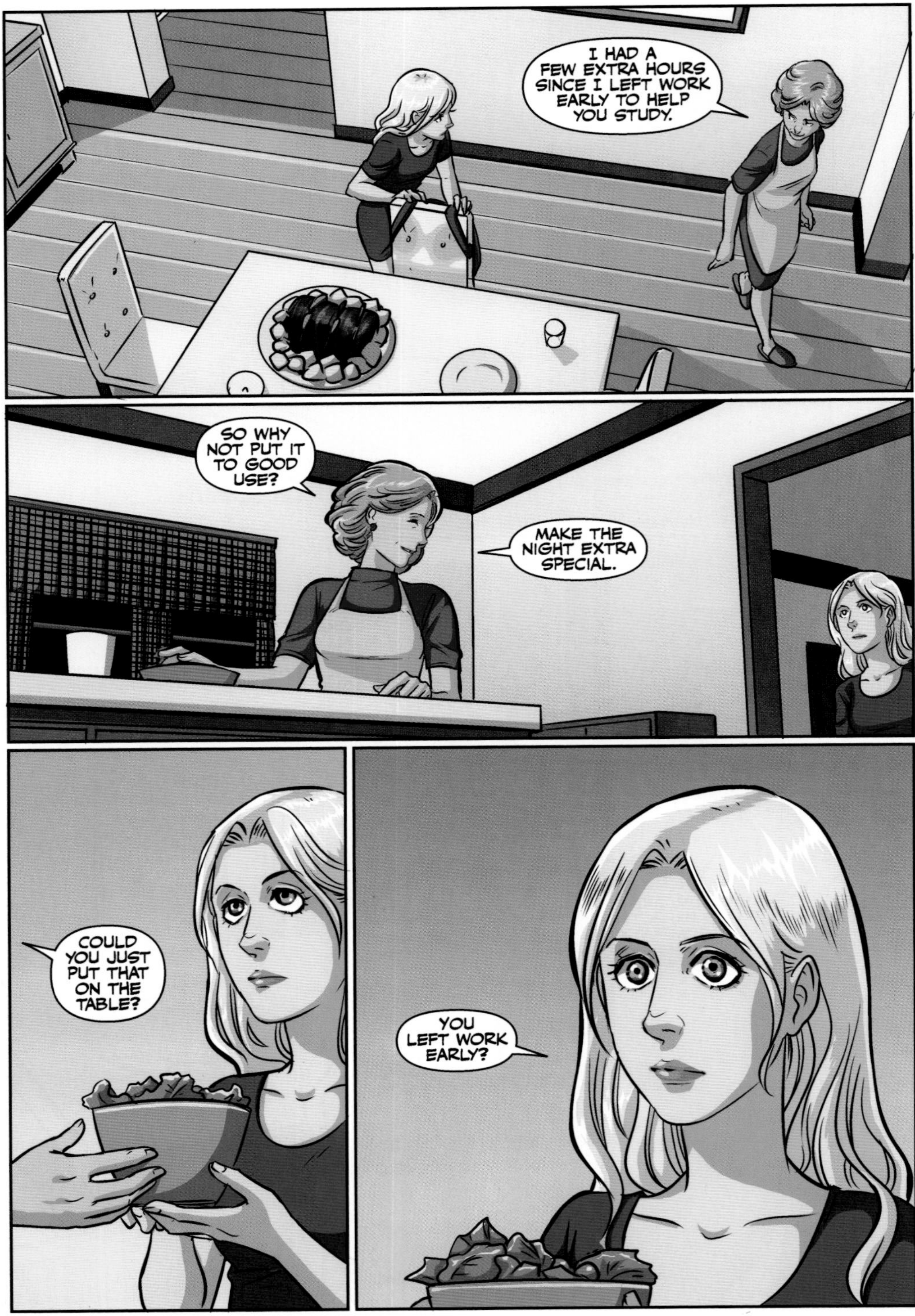
I HAD A FEW EXTRA HOURS SINCE I LEFT WORK EARLY TO HELP YOU STUDY.
SO WHY NOT PUT IT TO GOOD USE?
MAKE THE NIGHT EXTRA SPECIAL.
COULD YOU JUST PUT THAT ON THE TABLE?
YOU LEFT WORK EARLY?

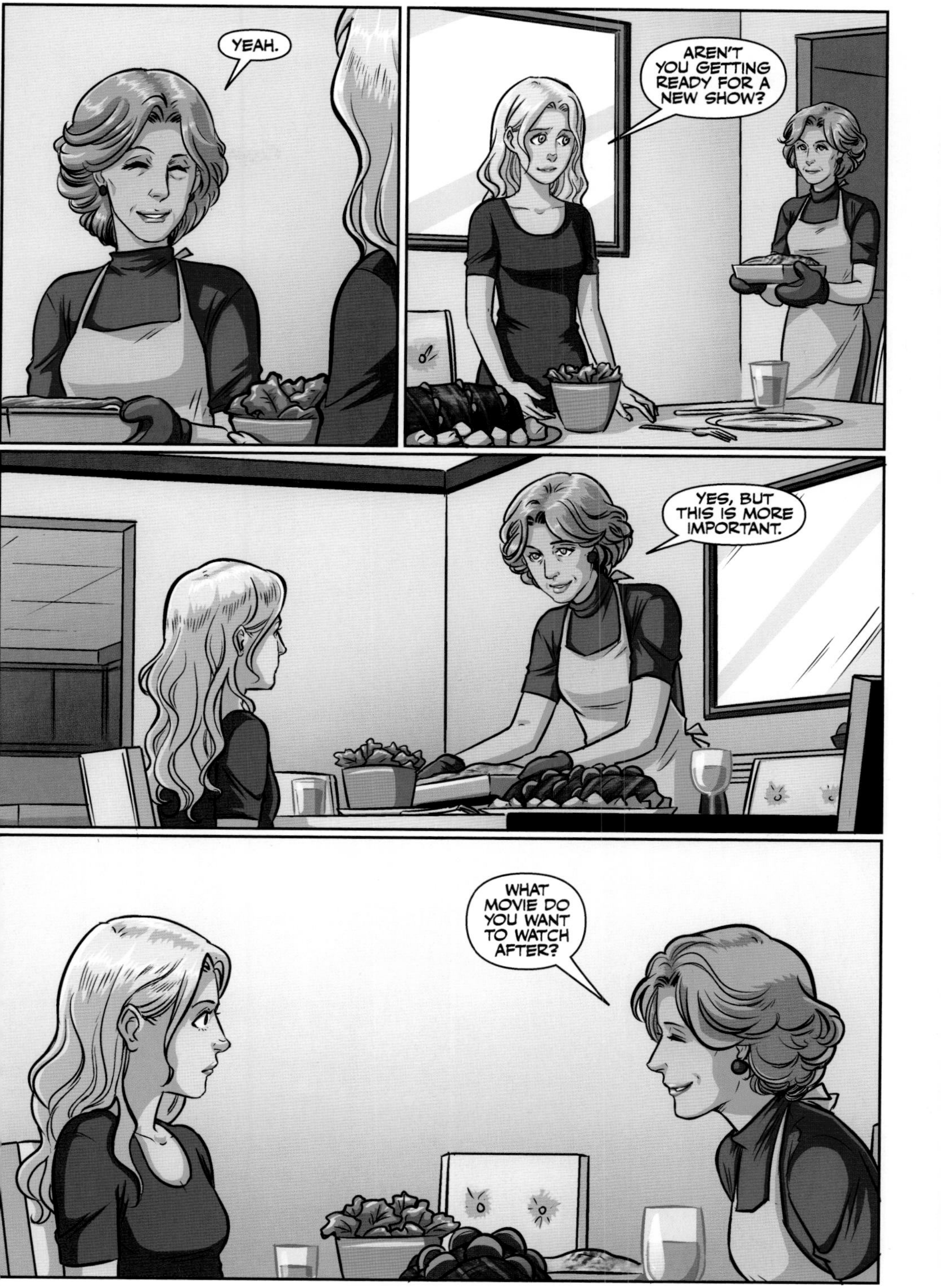
YEAH.
AREN'T YOU GETTING READY FOR A NEW SHOW?
YES, BUT THIS IS MORE IMPORTANT.
WHAT MOVIE DO YOU WANT TO WATCH AFTER?

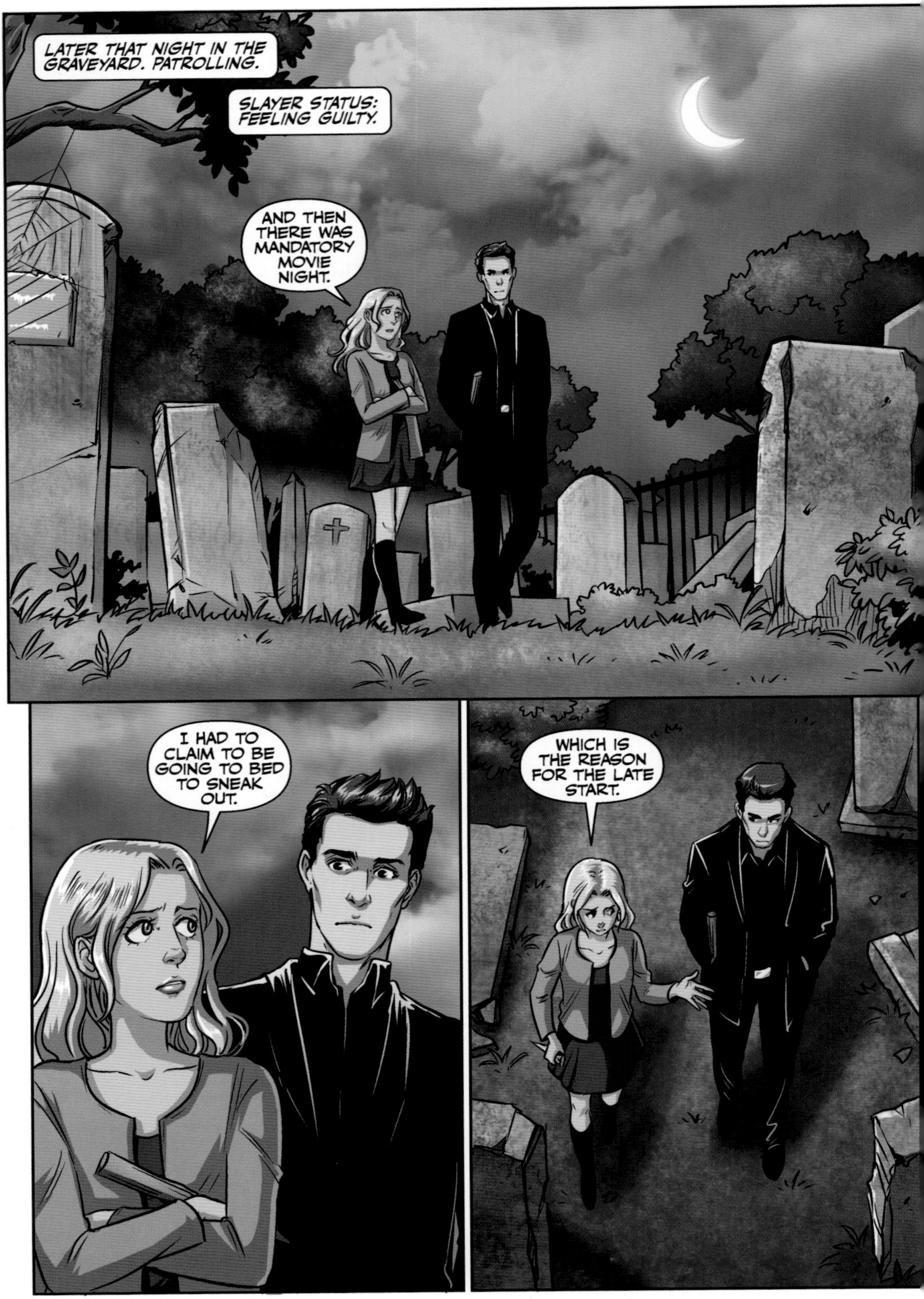
LATER THAT NIGHT IN THE GRAVEYARD. PATROLLING.
SLAYER STATUS: FEELING GUILTY.
AND THEN THERE WAS MANDATORY MOVIE NIGHT.
I HAD TO CLAIM TO BE GOING TO BED TO SNEAK OUT.
WHICH IS THE REASON FOR THE LATE START.

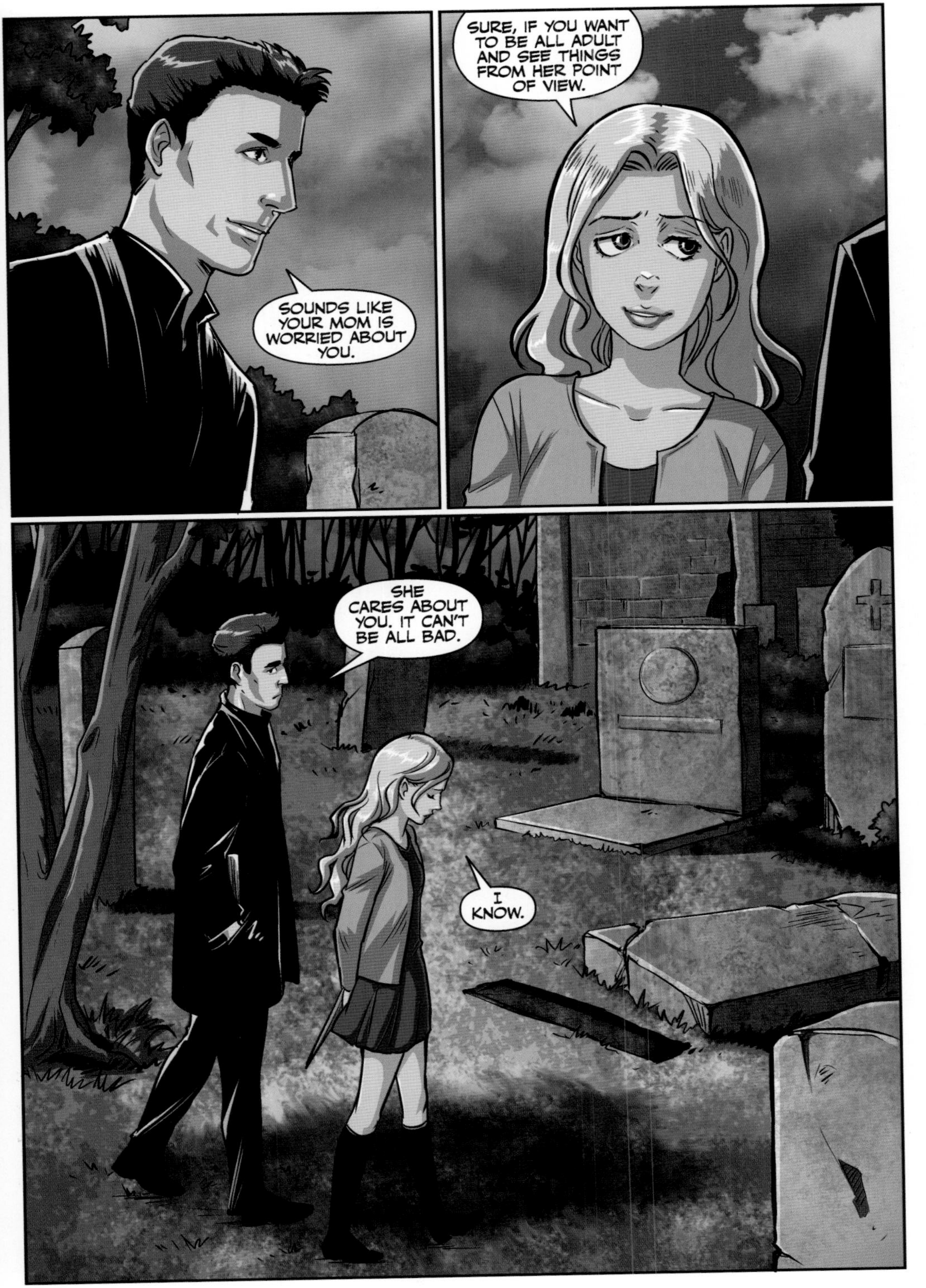
SOUNDS LIKE YOUR MOM IS WORRIED ABOUT YOU.
SURE, IF YOU WANT TO BE ALL ADULT AND SEE THINGS FROM HER POINT OF VIEW.
SHE CARES ABOUT YOU. IT CAN'T BE ALL BAD.
I KNOW.

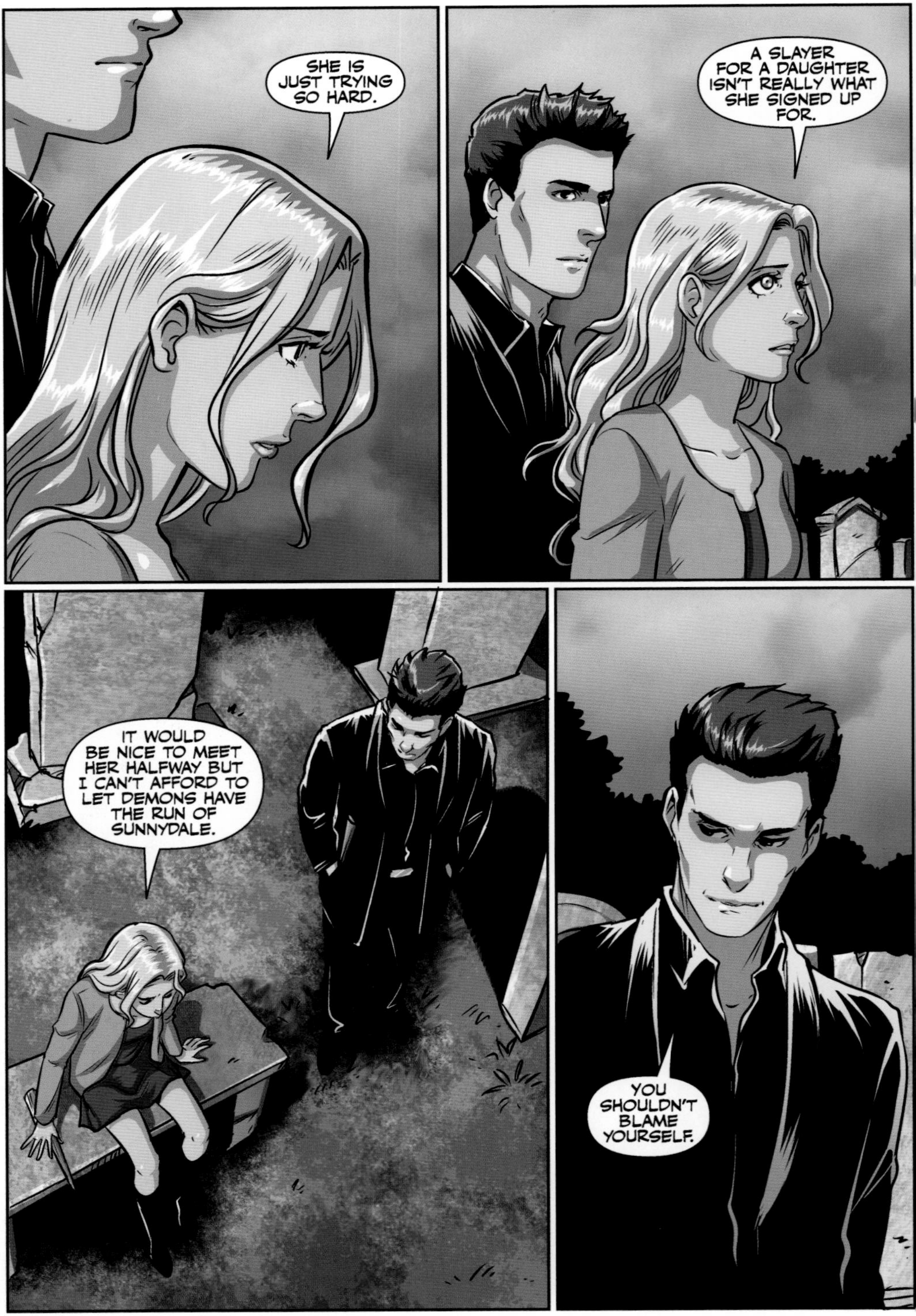
SHE IS JUST TRYING SO HARD.
A SLAYER FOR A DAUGHTER ISN'T REALLY WHAT SHE SIGNED UP FOR.
IT WOULD BE NICE TO MEET HER HALFWAY BUT I CAN'T AFFORD TO LET DEMONS HAVE THE RUN OF SUNNYDALE.
YOU SHOULDN'T BLAME YOURSELF.

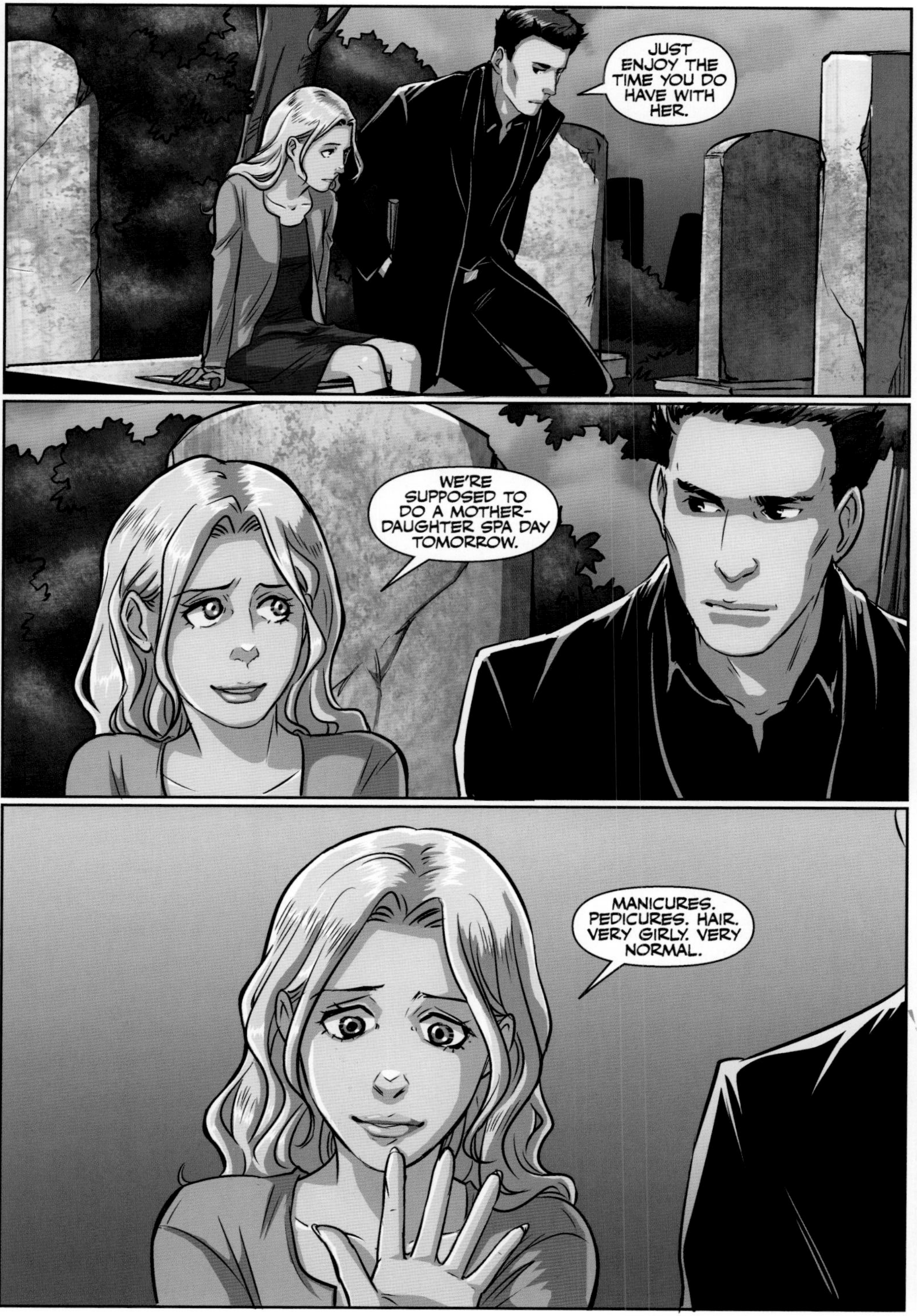
JUST ENJOY THE TIME YOU DO HAVE WITH HER.
WE'RE SUPPOSED TO DO A MOTHER-DAUGHTER SPA DAY TOMORROW.
MANICURES. PEDICURES. HAIR. VERY GIRLY. VERY NORMAL.

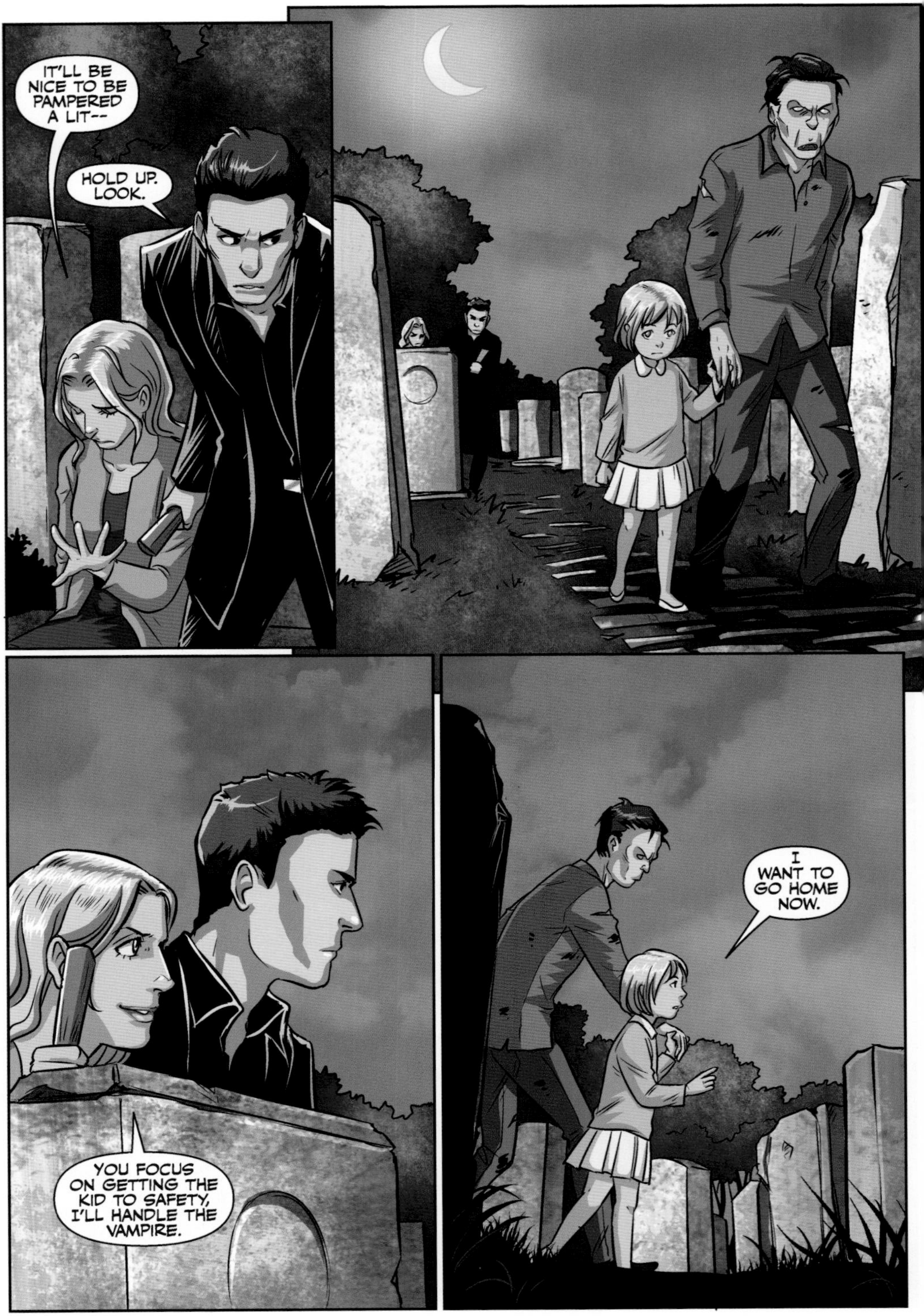
IT'LL BE NICE TO BE PAMPERED A LIT--
HOLD UP. LOOK.
YOU FOCUS ON GETTING THE KID TO SAFETY, I'LL HANDLE THE VAMPIRE.
I WANT TO GO HOME NOW.

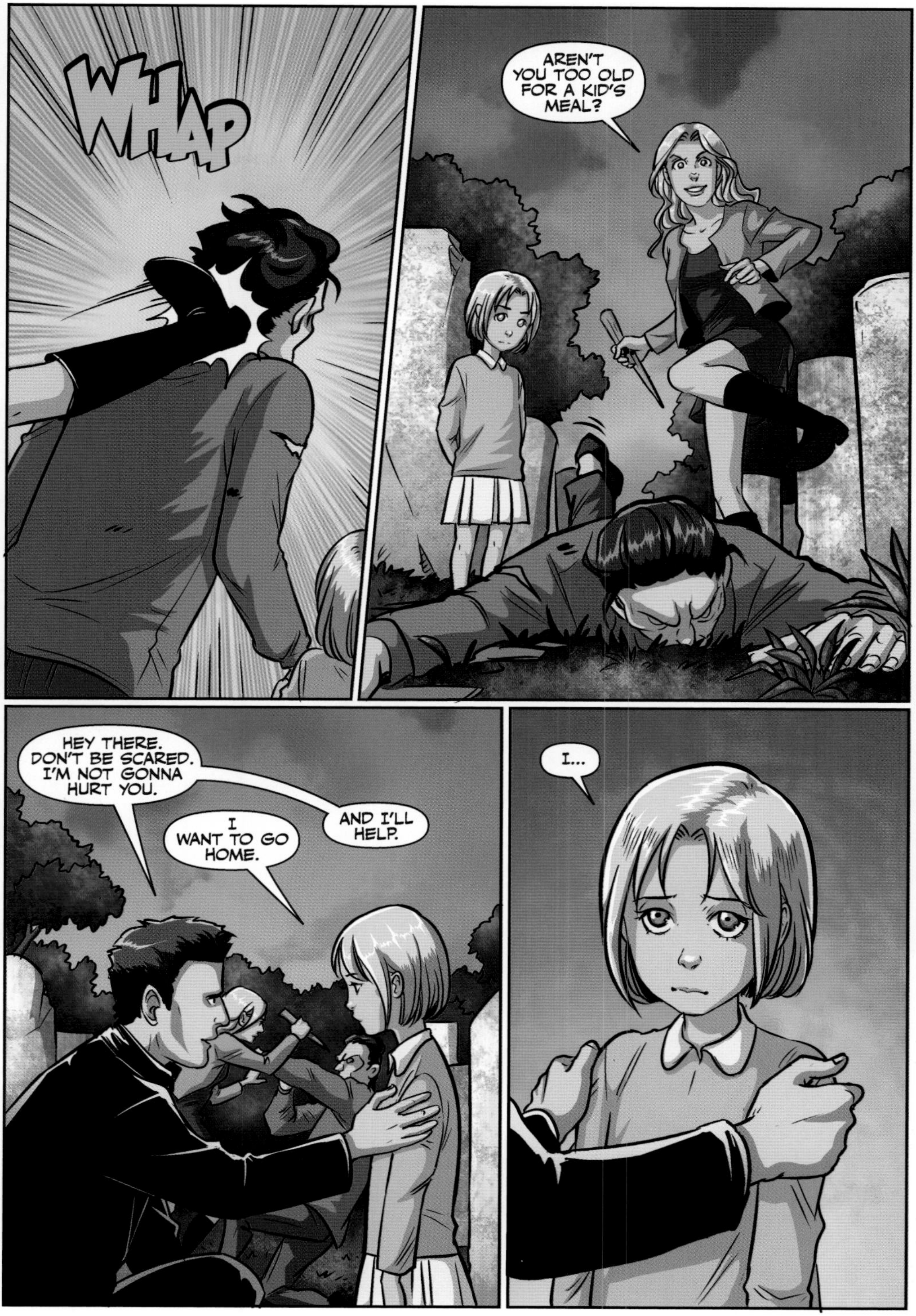
WHAP
AREN'T YOU TOO OLD FOR A KID'S MEAL?
HEY THERE. DON'T BE SCARED. I'M NOT GONNA HURT YOU.
AND I'LL HELP.
I WANT TO GO HOME.
I...

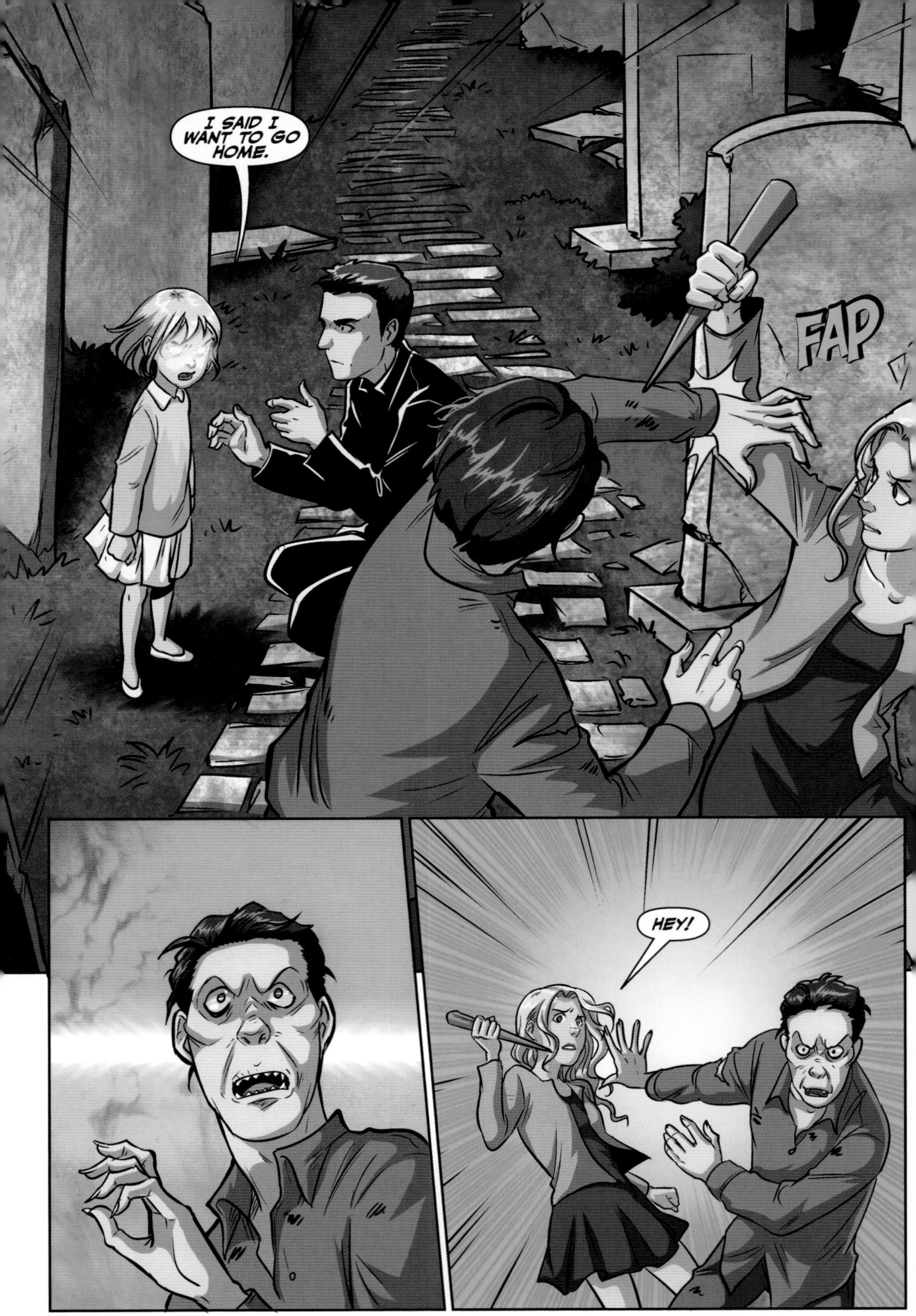
I SAID I WANT TO GO HOME.
FAP
HEY!

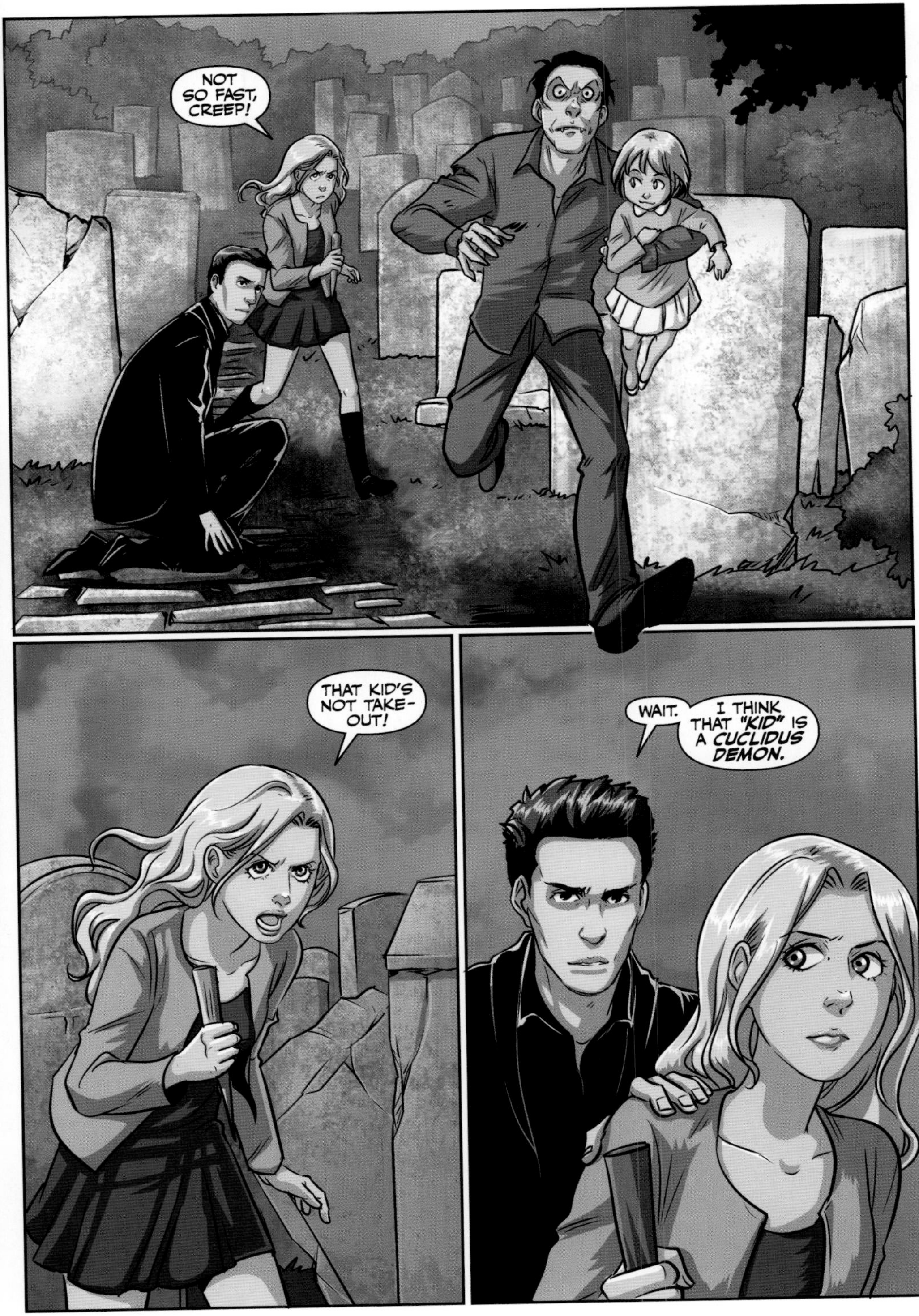
NOT SO FAST, CREEP!
THAT KID'S NOT TAKE-OUT!
WAIT.
I THINK THAT "KID" IS A CUCLIDUS DEMON.

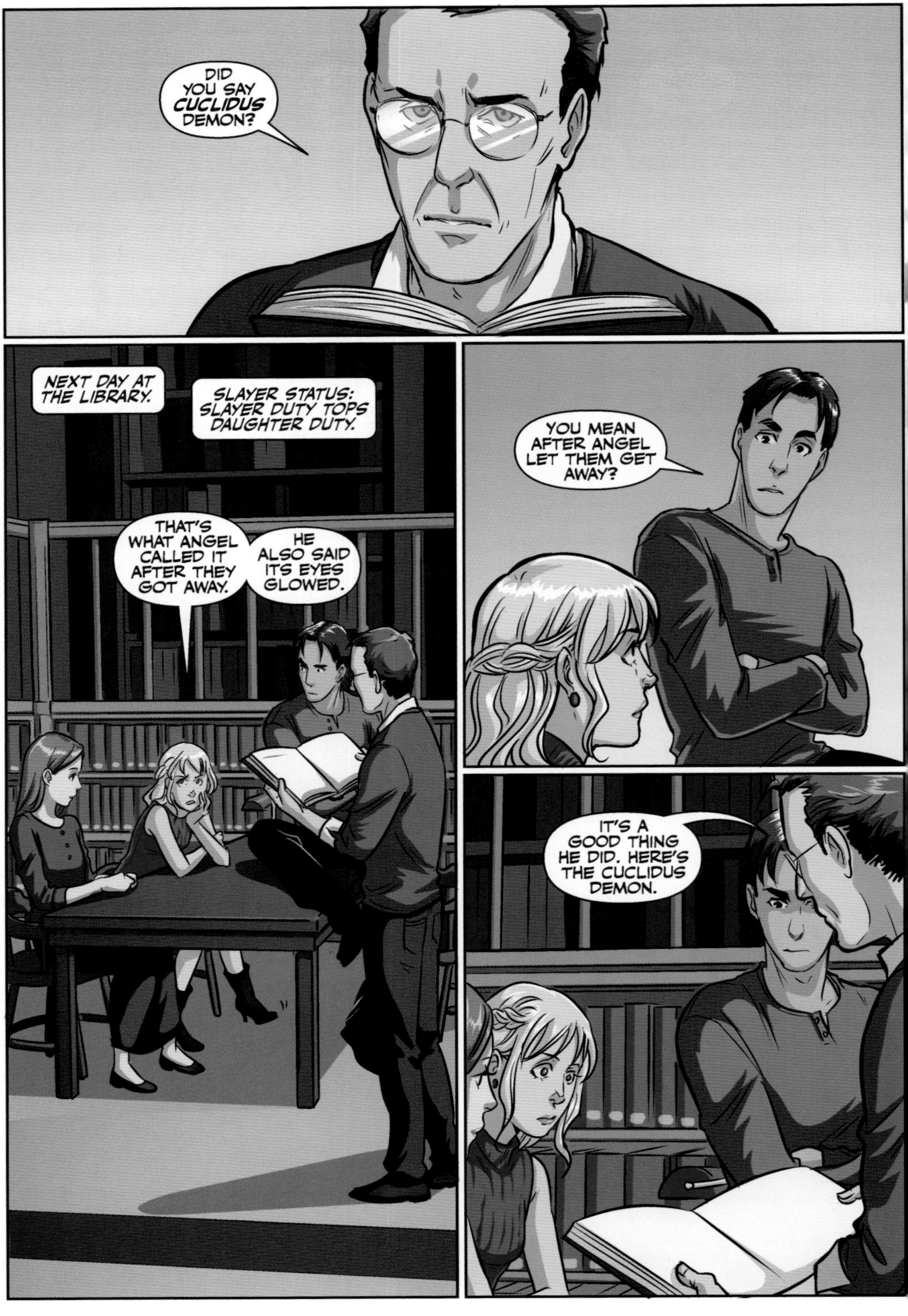
DID YOU SAY *CUCLIDUS* DEMON?
NEXT DAY AT THE LIBRARY.
SLAYER STATUS: SLAYER DUTY TOPS DAUGHTER DUTY.
THAT'S WHAT ANGEL CALLED IT AFTER THEY GOT AWAY.
HE ALSO SAID ITS EYES GLOWED.
YOU MEAN AFTER ANGEL LET THEM GET AWAY?
IT'S A GOOD THING HE DID. HERE'S THE CUCLIDUS DEMON.

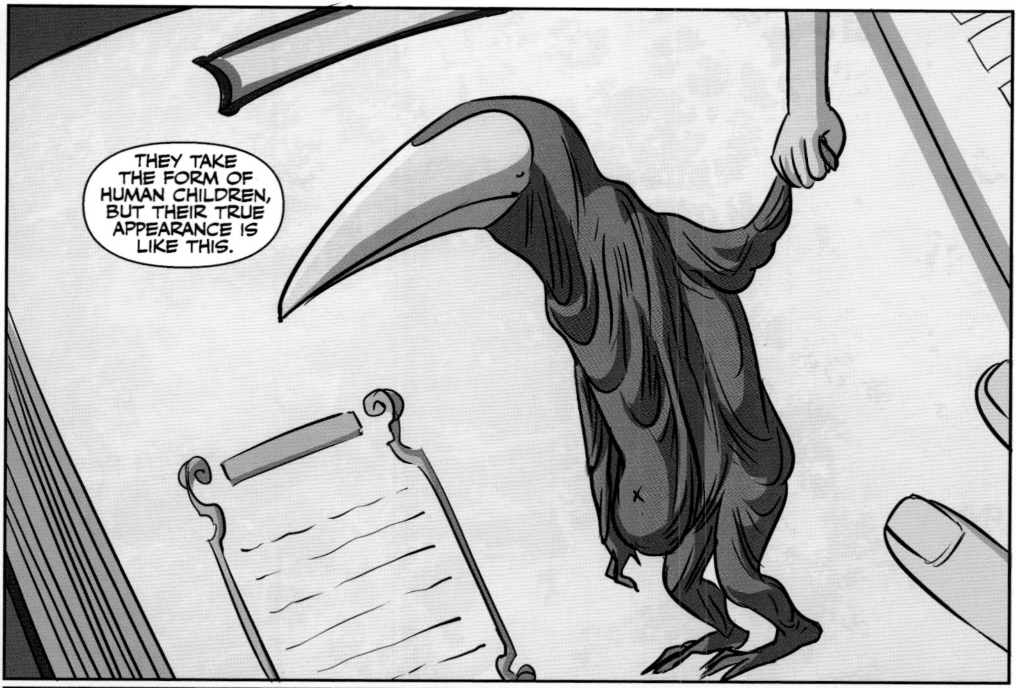
THEY TAKE THE FORM OF HUMAN CHILDREN, BUT THEIR TRUE APPEARANCE IS LIKE THIS.

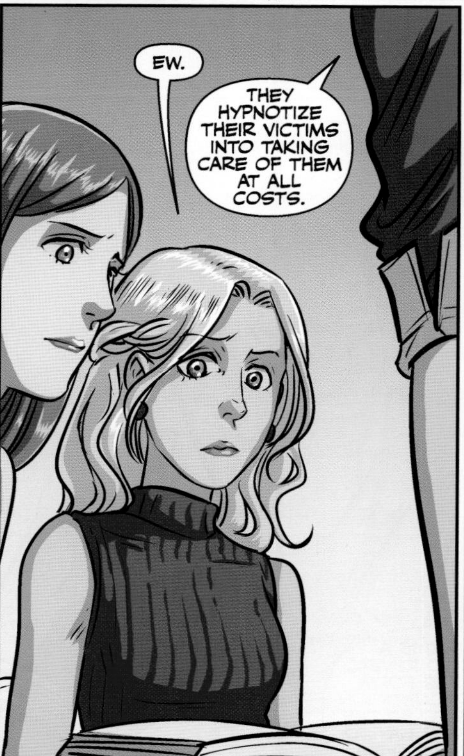
EW.
THEY HYPNOTIZE THEIR VICTIMS INTO TAKING CARE OF THEM AT ALL COSTS.

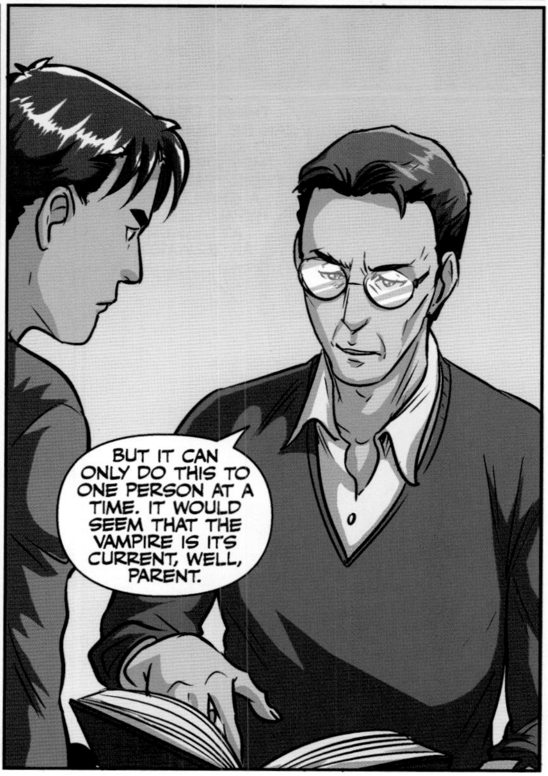
BUT IT CAN ONLY DO THIS TO ONE PERSON AT A TIME. IT WOULD SEEM THAT THE VAMPIRE IS ITS CURRENT, WELL, PARENT.

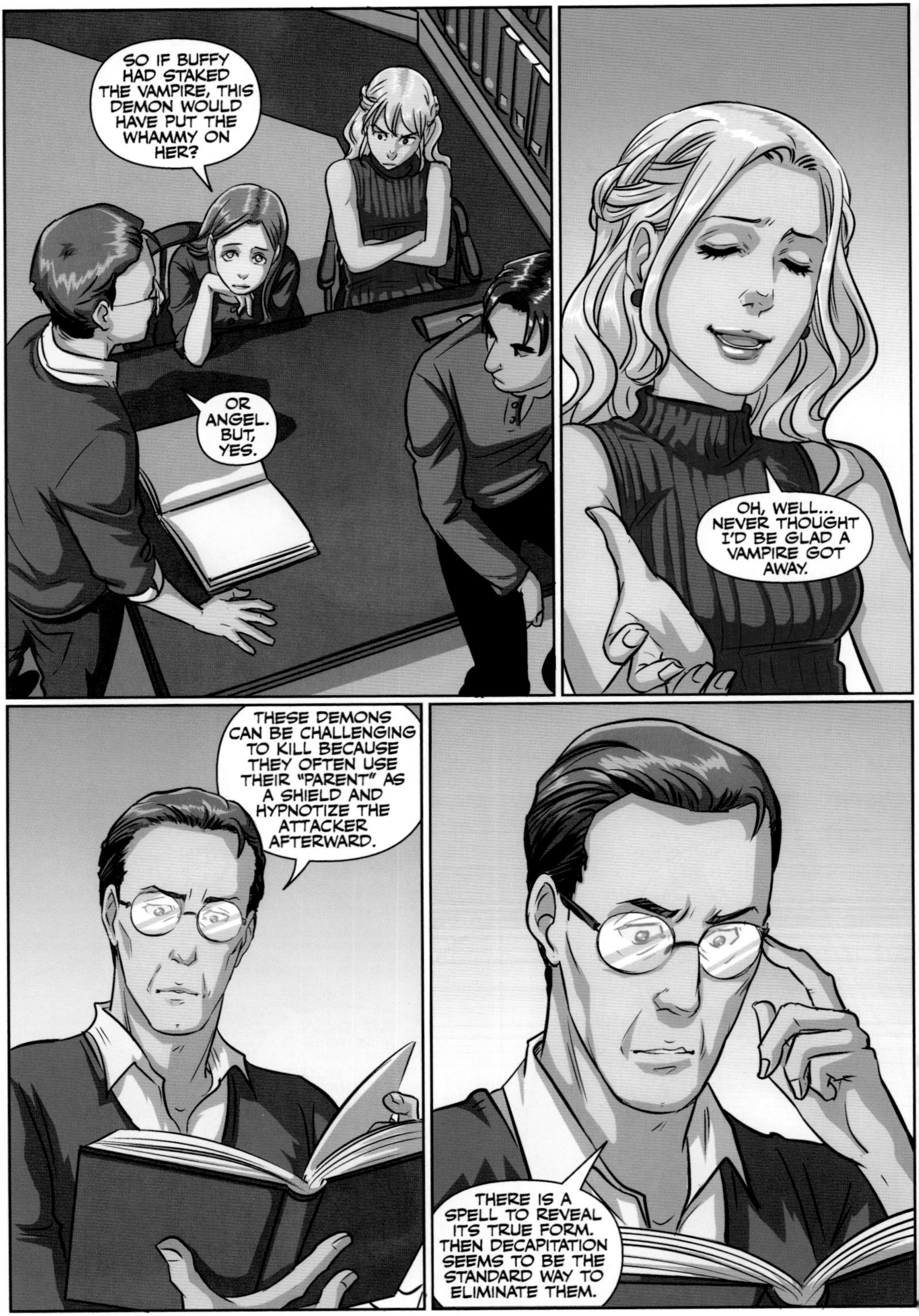
SO IF BUFFY HAD STAKED THE VAMPIRE, THIS DEMON WOULD HAVE PUT THE WHAMMY ON HER?
OR ANGEL. BUT, YES.
OH, WELL... NEVER THOUGHT I'D BE GLAD A VAMPIRE GOT AWAY.
THESE DEMONS CAN BE CHALLENGING TO KILL BECAUSE THEY OFTEN USE THEIR "PARENT" AS A SHIELD AND HYPNOTIZE THE ATTACKER AFTERWARD.
THERE IS A SPELL TO REVEAL ITS TRUE FORM. THEN DECAPITATION SEEMS TO BE THE STANDARD WAY TO ELIMINATE THEM.

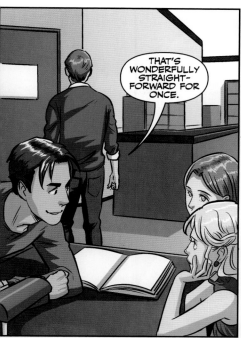

THAT'S WONDERFULLY STRAIGHT-FORWARD FOR ONCE.

SLICE AND DICE THE DEMON. THEN SLICE AND DICE THE VAMPIRE.

BUT WE STILL HAVE TO FIND IT.

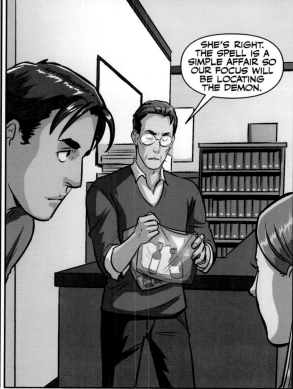

SHE'S RIGHT. THE SPELL IS A SIMPLE AFFAIR SO OUR FOCUS WILL BE LOCATING THE DEMON.

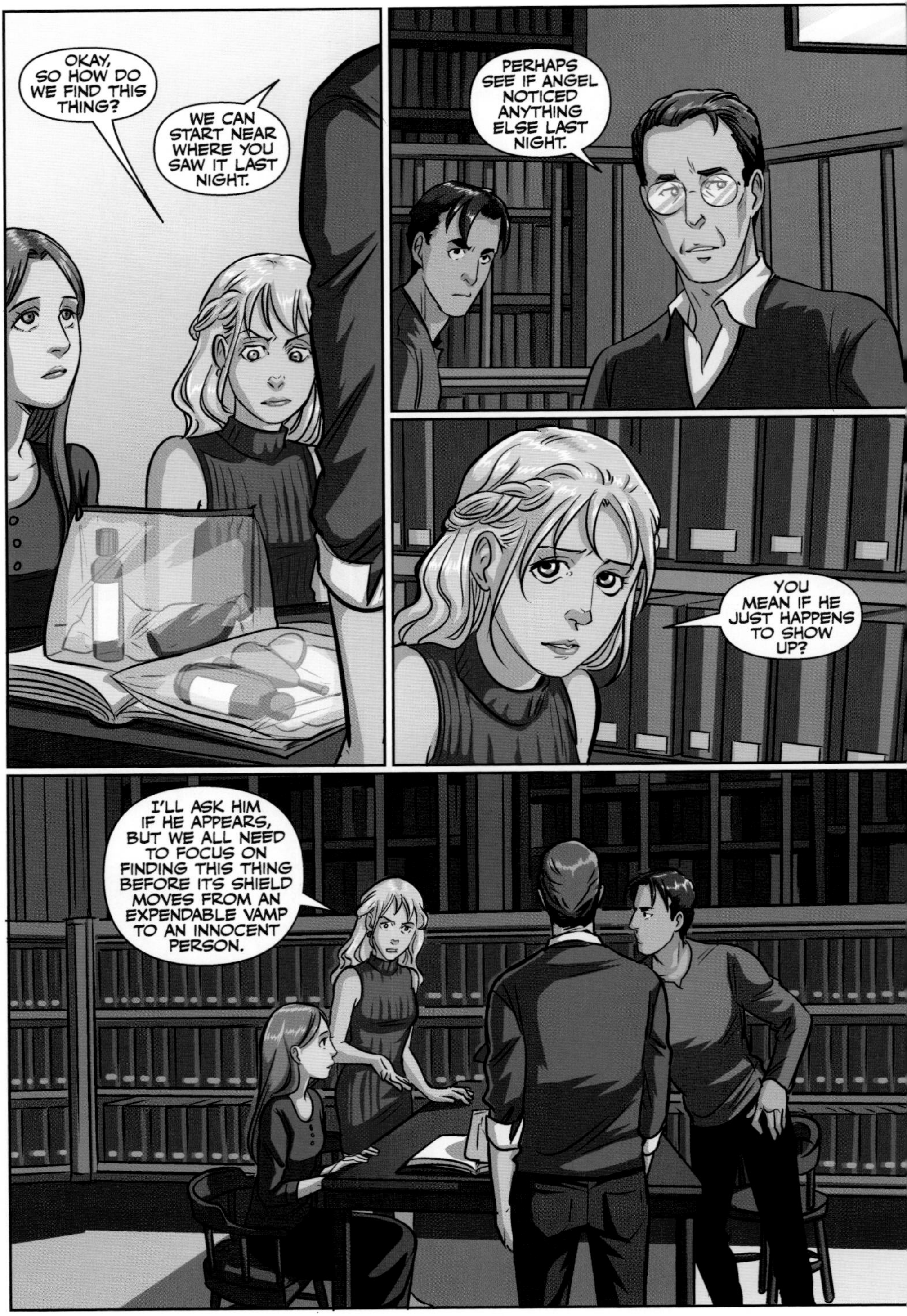
OKAY, SO HOW DO WE FIND THIS THING?
WE CAN START NEAR WHERE YOU SAW IT LAST NIGHT.
PERHAPS SEE IF ANGEL NOTICED ANYTHING ELSE LAST NIGHT.
YOU MEAN IF HE JUST HAPPENS TO SHOW UP?
I'LL ASK HIM IF HE APPEARS, BUT WE ALL NEED TO FOCUS ON FINDING THIS THING BEFORE ITS SHIELD MOVES FROM AN EXPENDABLE VAMP TO AN INNOCENT PERSON.

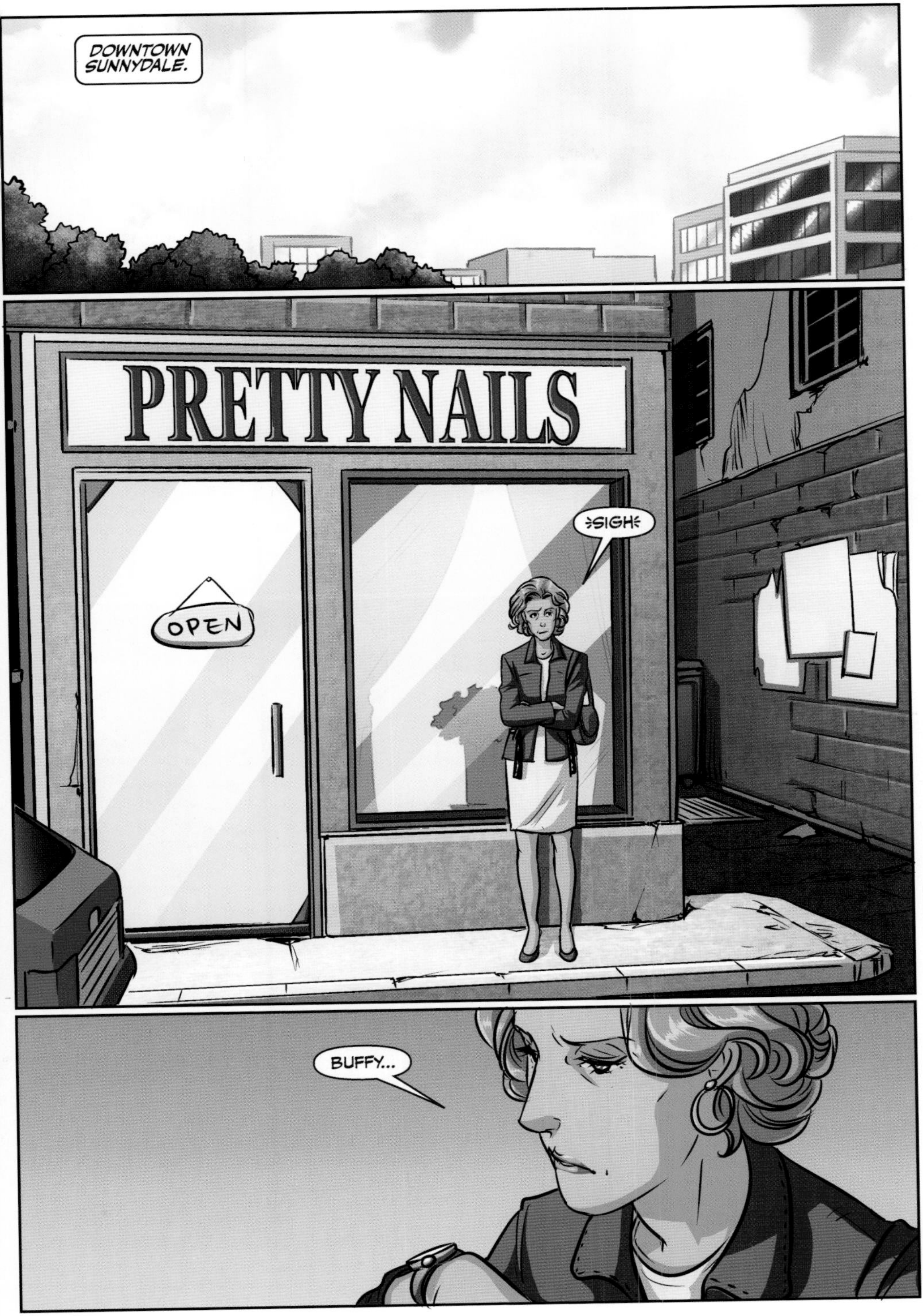
DOWNTOWN SUNNYDALE.
PRETTY NAILS
OPEN
SIGH
BUFFY...

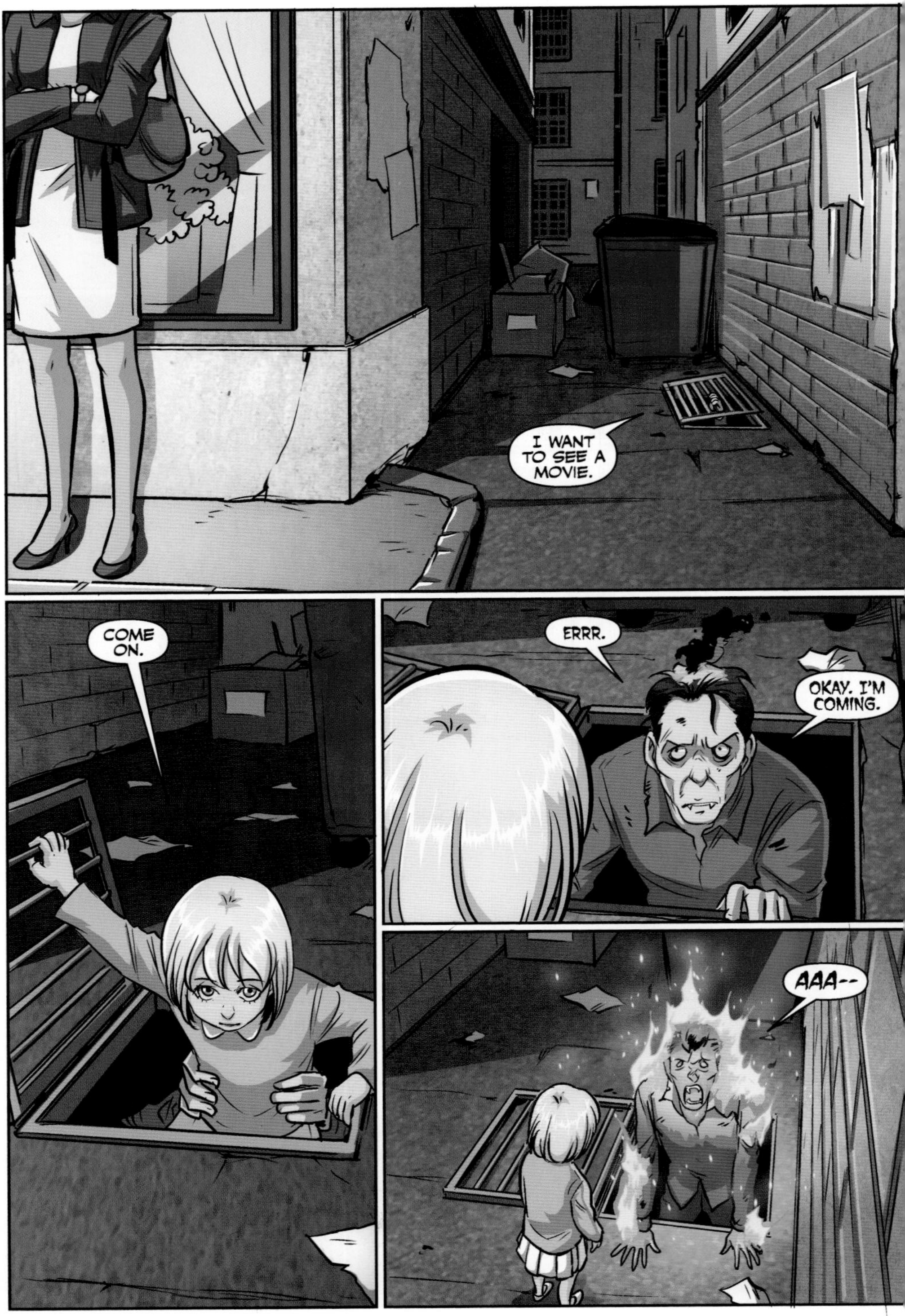
I WANT TO SEE A MOVIE.
COME ON.
ERRR.
OKAY. I'M COMING.
AAA--

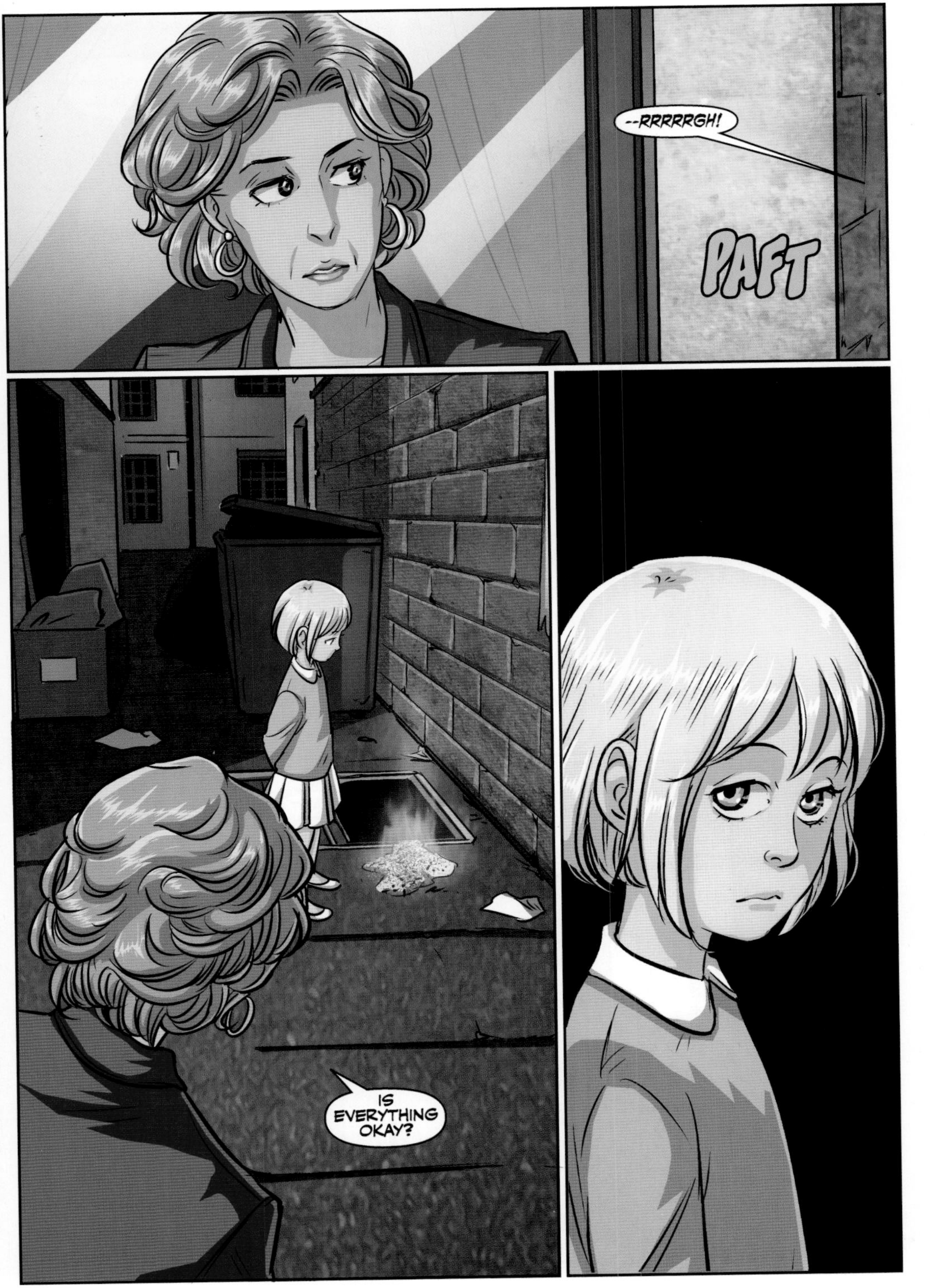
--RRRRRGH!
PAFT
IS EVERYTHING OKAY?

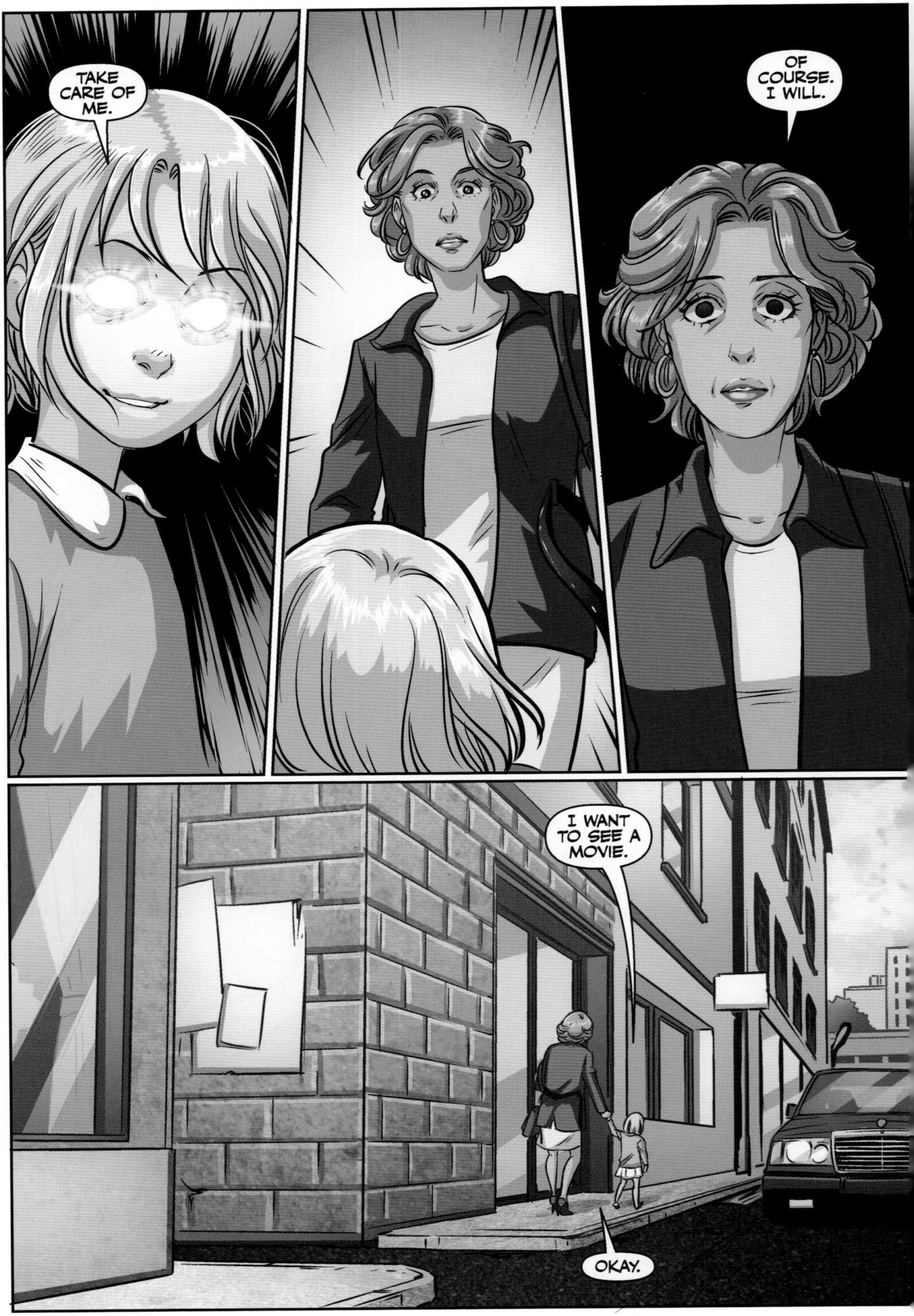
TAKE CARE OF ME.
OF COURSE. I WILL.
I WANT TO SEE A MOVIE.
OKAY.

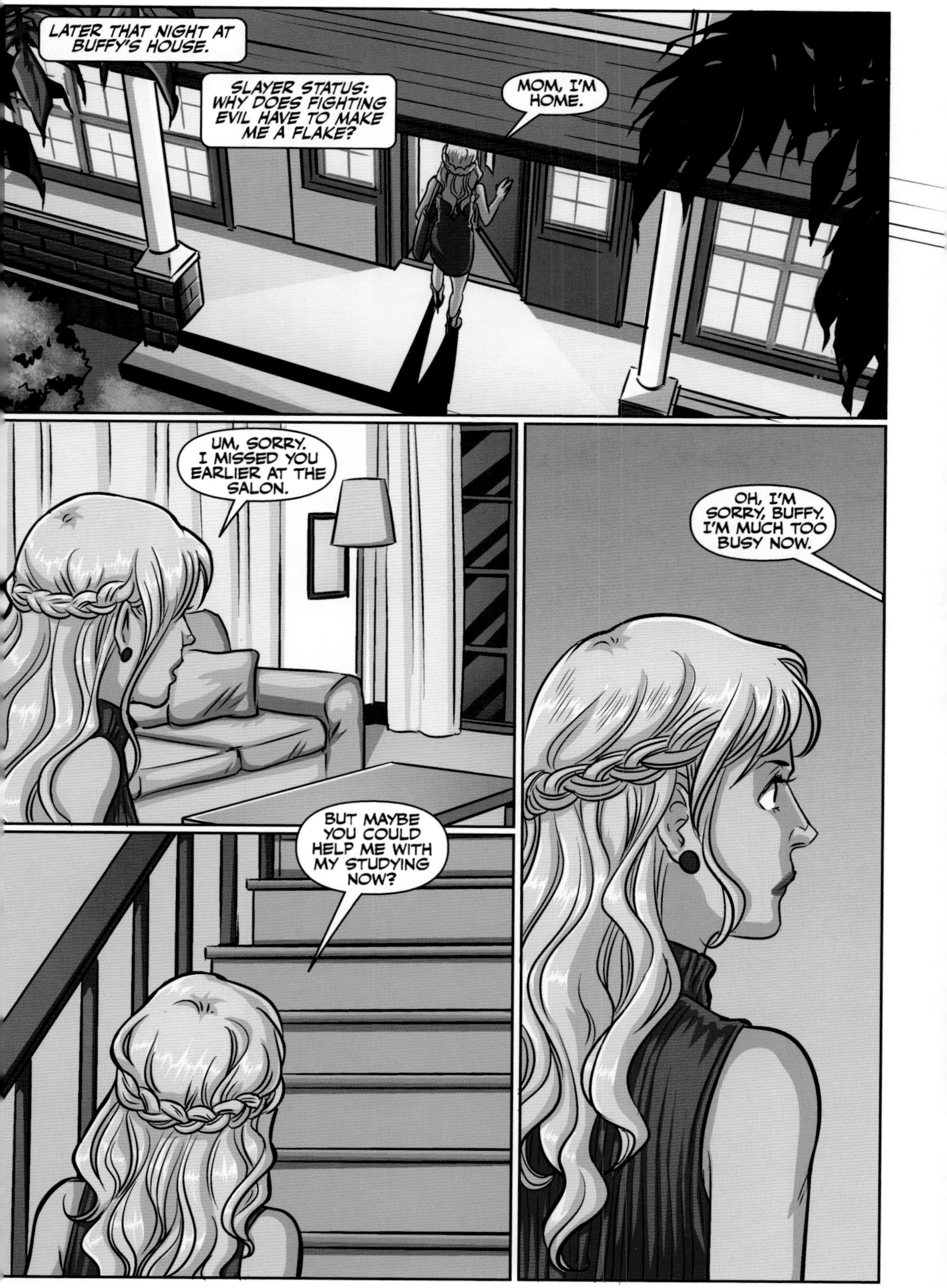
LATER THAT NIGHT AT BUFFY'S HOUSE.
SLAYER STATUS: WHY DOES FIGHTING EVIL HAVE TO MAKE ME A FLAKE?
MOM, I'M HOME.
UM, SORRY. I MISSED YOU EARLIER AT THE SALON.
OH, I'M SORRY, BUFFY. I'M MUCH TOO BUSY NOW.
BUT MAYBE YOU COULD HELP ME WITH MY STUDYING NOW?

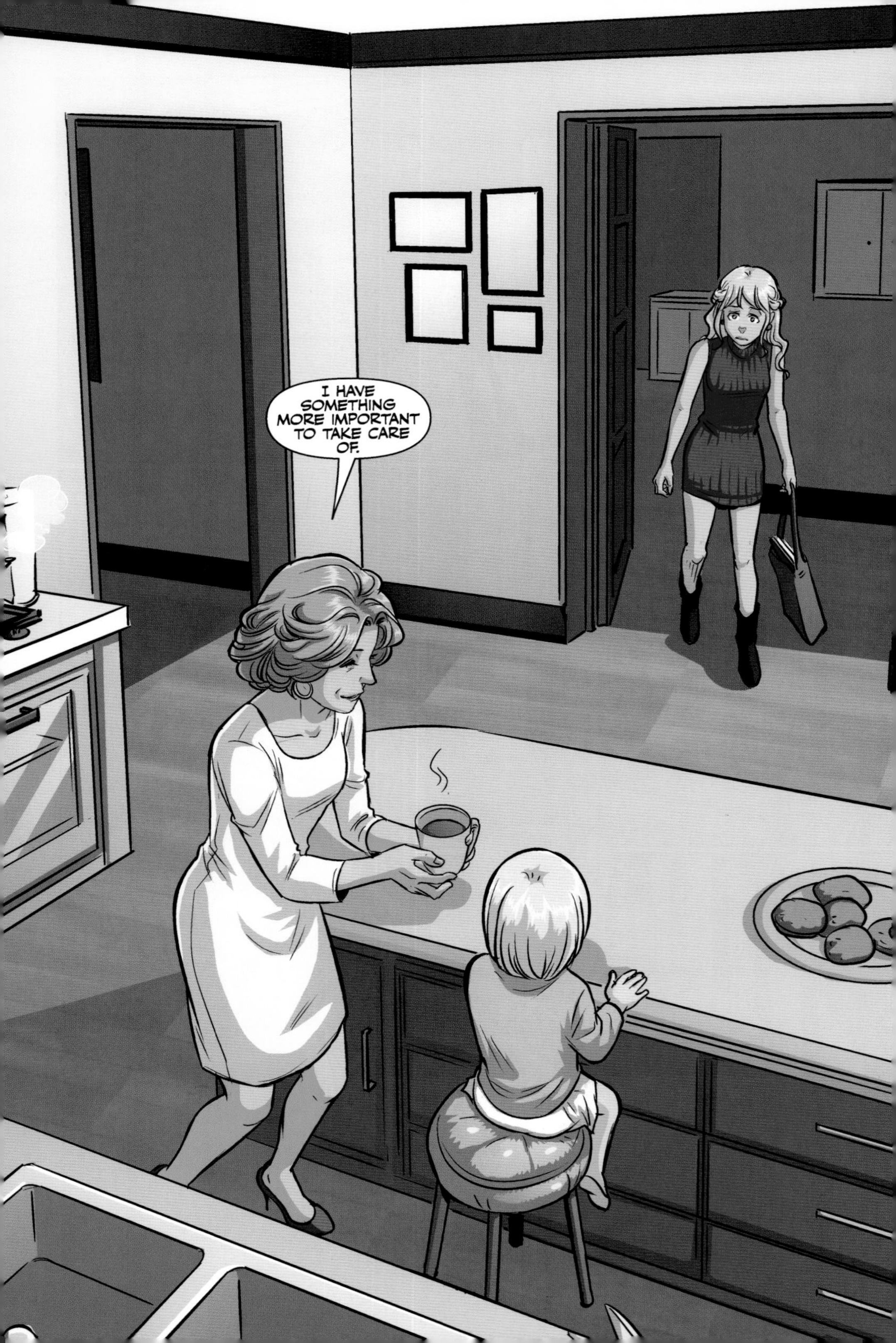
I HAVE SOMETHING MORE IMPORTANT TO TAKE CARE OF.

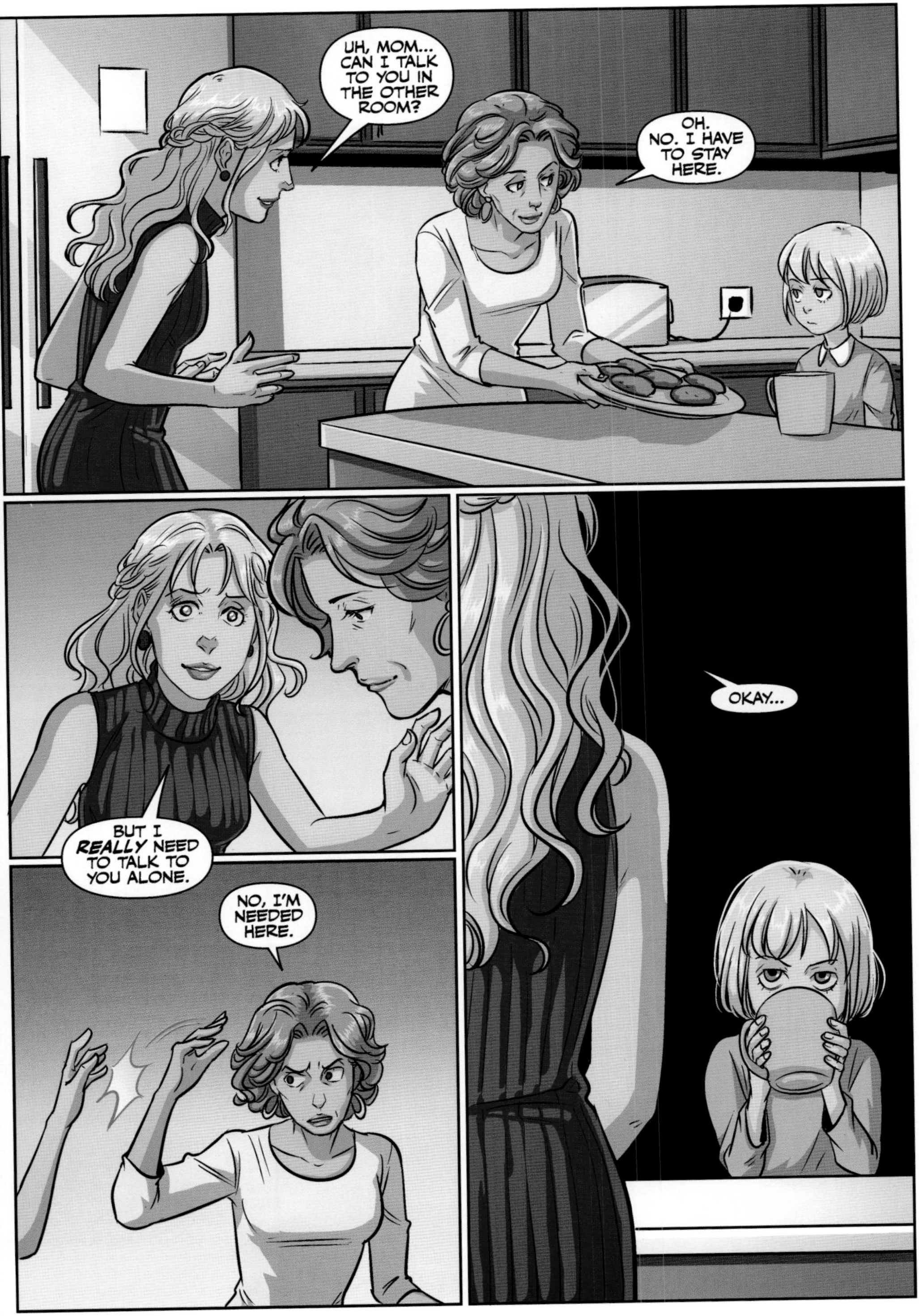
UH, MOM... CAN I TALK TO YOU IN THE OTHER ROOM?
OH. NO. I HAVE TO STAY HERE.
BUT I REALLY NEED TO TALK TO YOU ALONE.
NO, I'M NEEDED HERE.
OKAY...

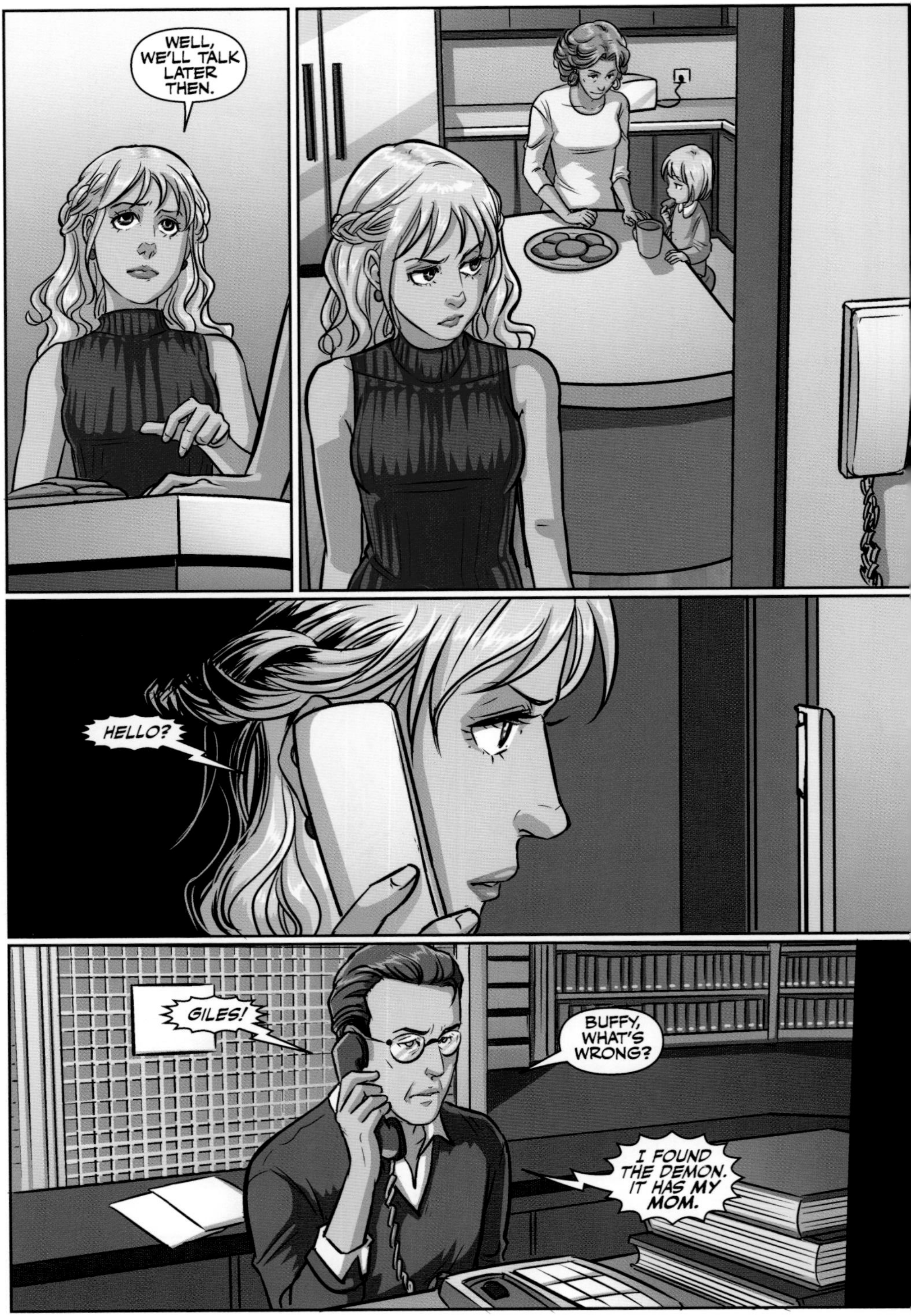
WELL, WE'LL TALK LATER THEN.
HELLO?
GILES!
BUFFY, WHAT'S WRONG?
I FOUND THE DEMON. IT HAS MY MOM.

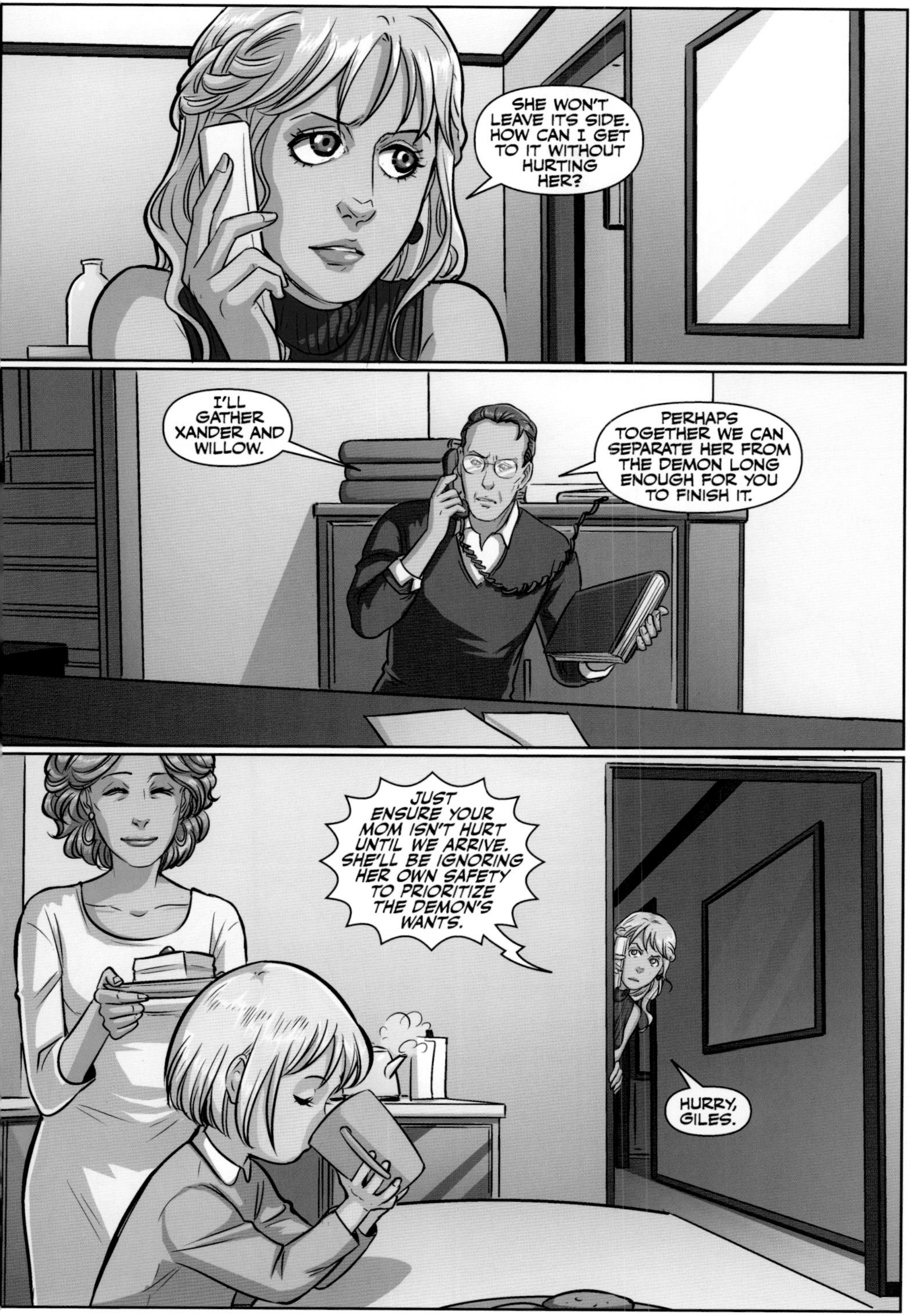
SHE WON'T LEAVE ITS SIDE. HOW CAN I GET TO IT WITHOUT HURTING HER?
I'LL GATHER XANDER AND WILLOW.
PERHAPS TOGETHER WE CAN SEPARATE HER FROM THE DEMON LONG ENOUGH FOR YOU TO FINISH IT.
JUST ENSURE YOUR MOM ISN'T HURT UNTIL WE ARRIVE. SHE'LL BE IGNORING HER OWN SAFETY TO PRIORITIZE THE DEMON'S WANTS.
HURRY, GILES.

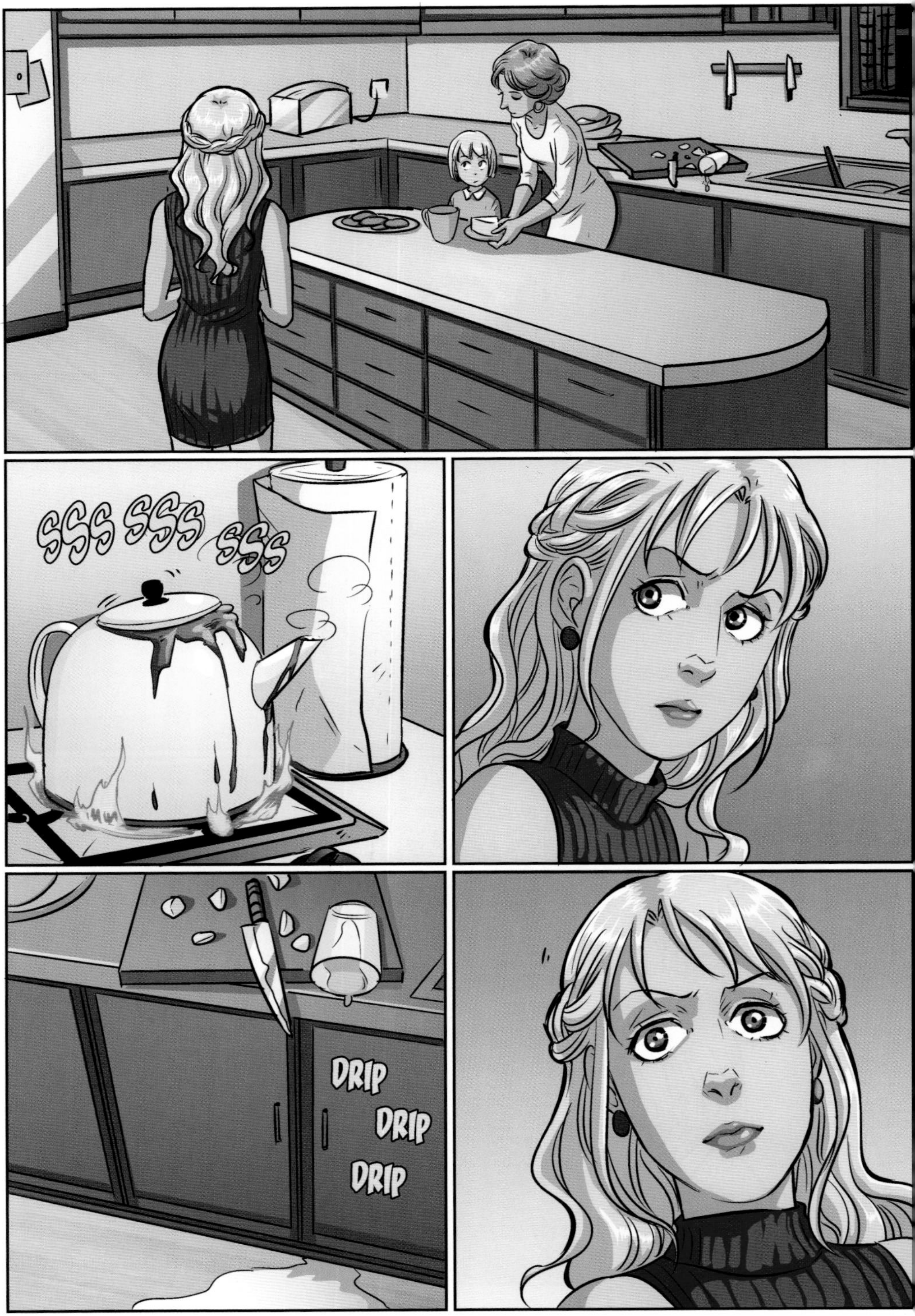
SSS SSS SSS
DRIP
DRIP
DRIP

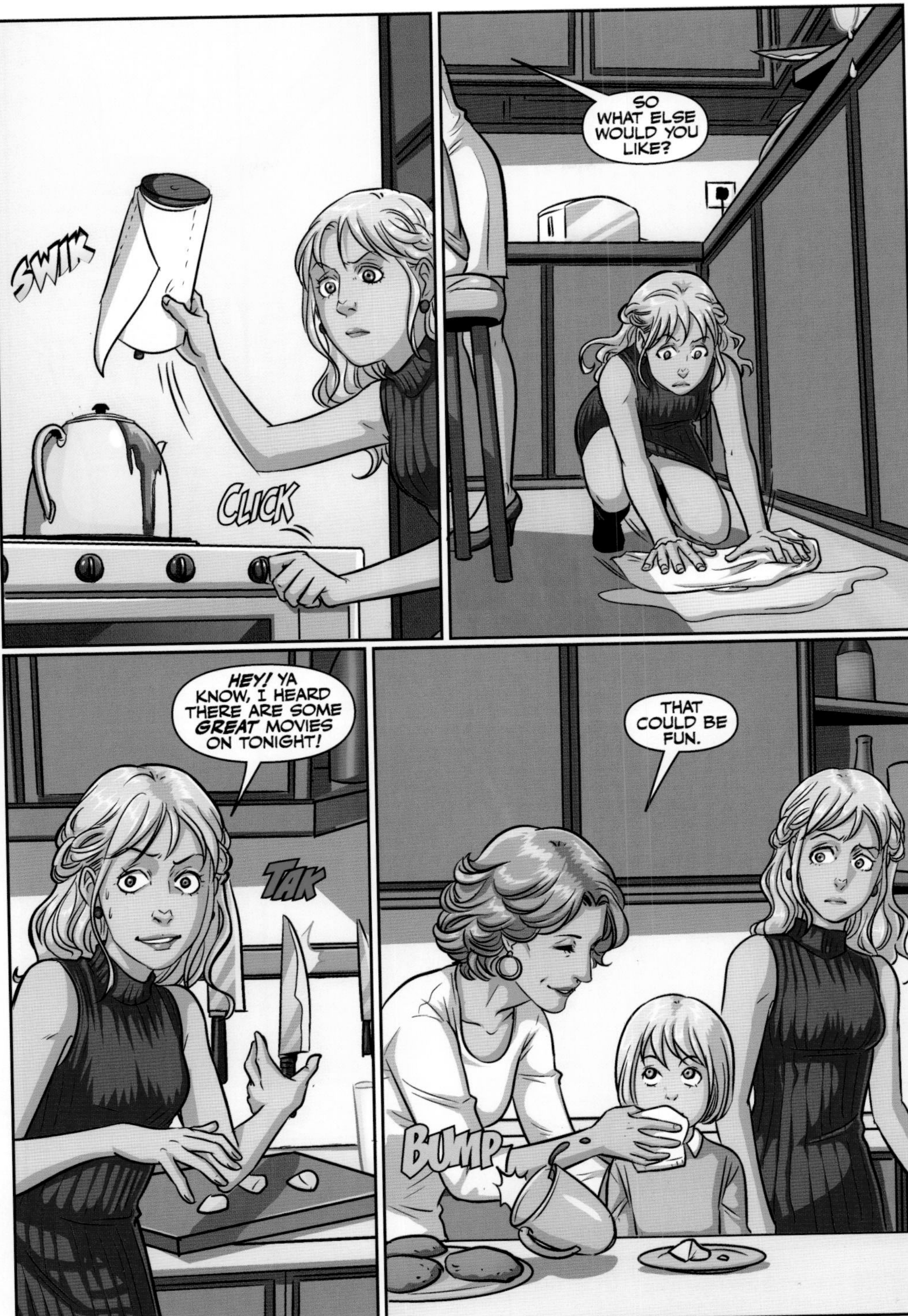
SWIK
CLICK
SO WHAT ELSE WOULD YOU LIKE?
HEY! YA KNOW, I HEARD THERE ARE SOME GREAT MOVIES ON TONIGHT!
TAK
THAT COULD BE FUN.
BUMP

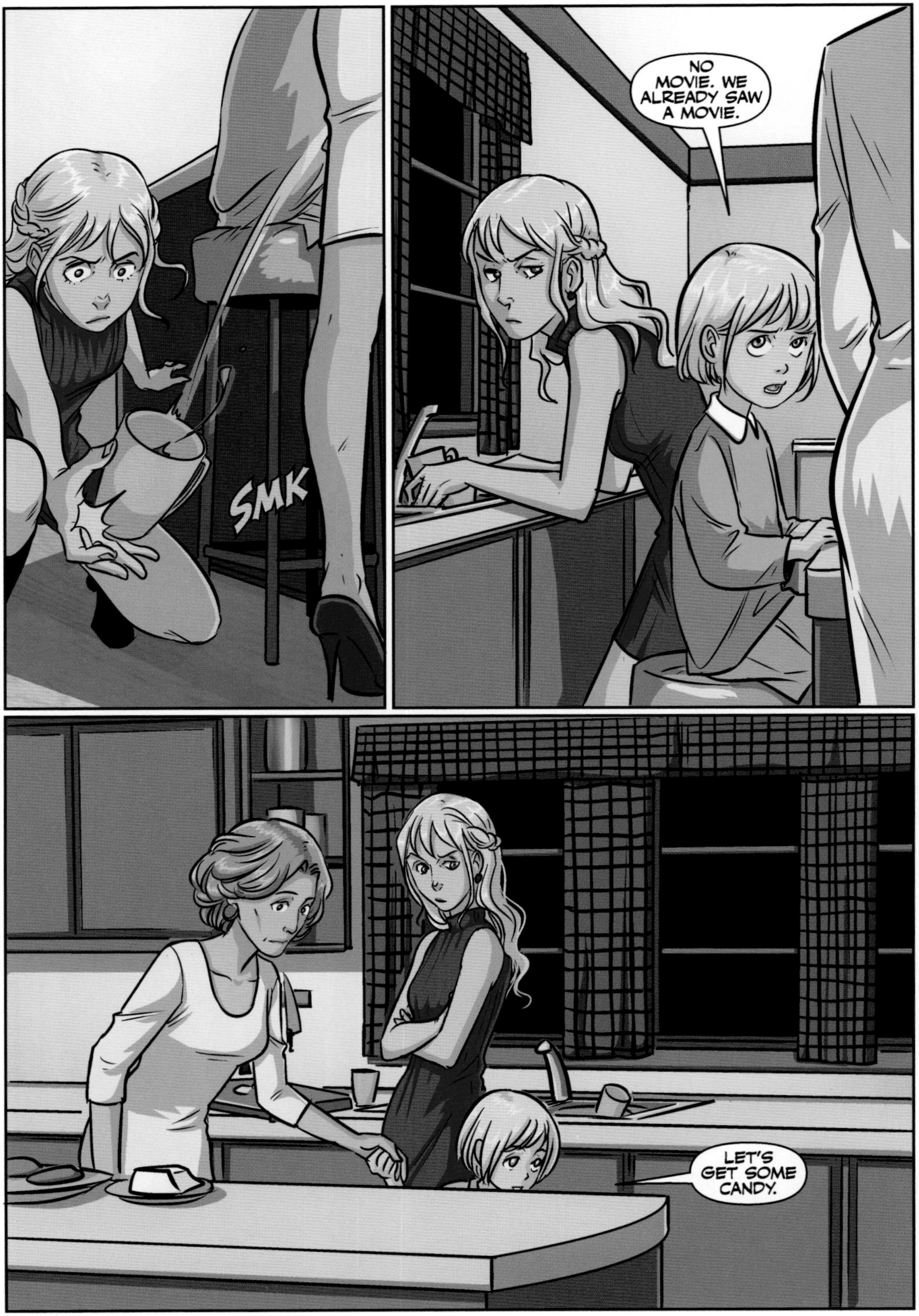
SMK
NO MOVIE. WE ALREADY SAW A MOVIE.
LET'S GET SOME CANDY.

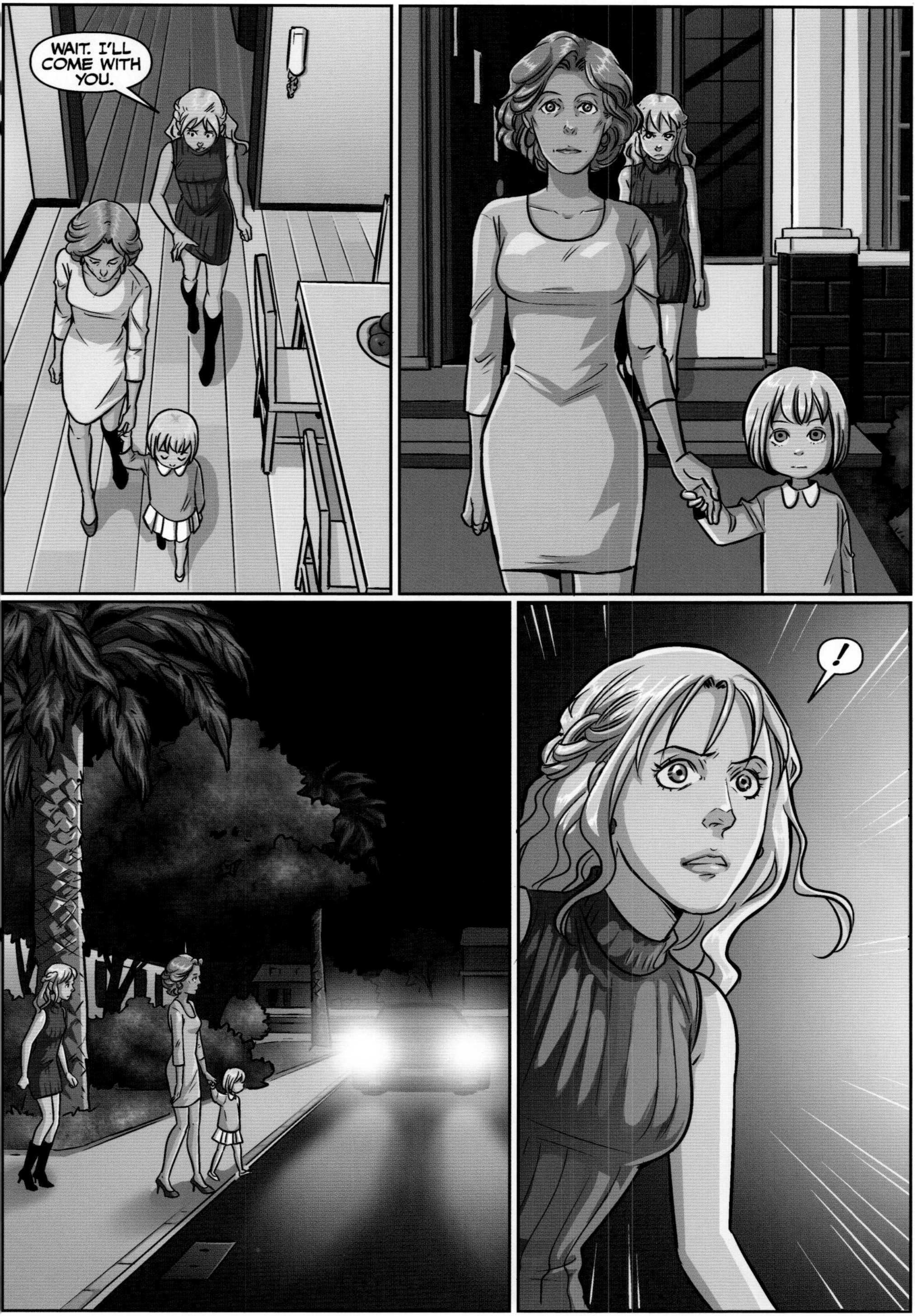
WAIT. I'LL COME WITH YOU.
!

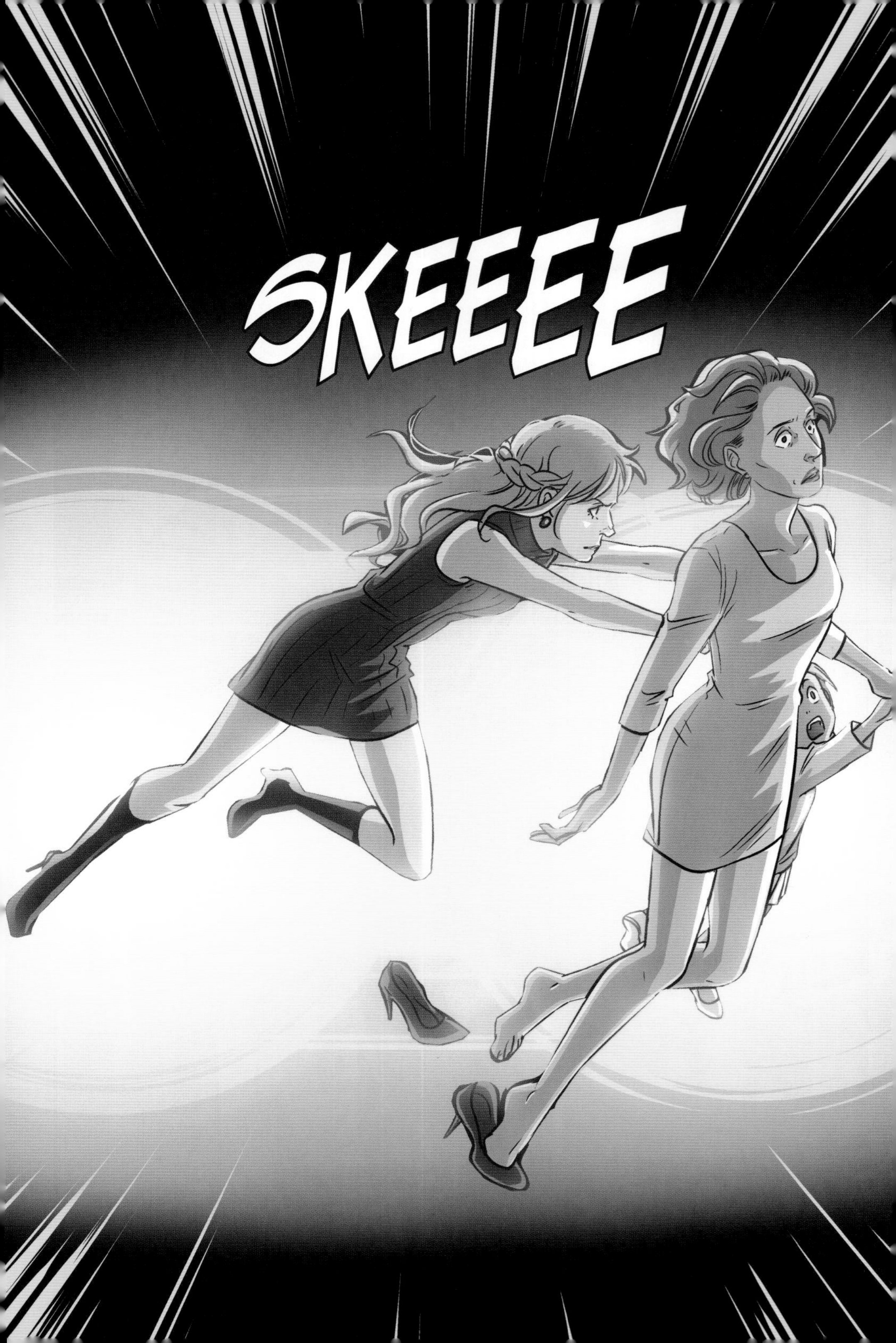
SKEEEE

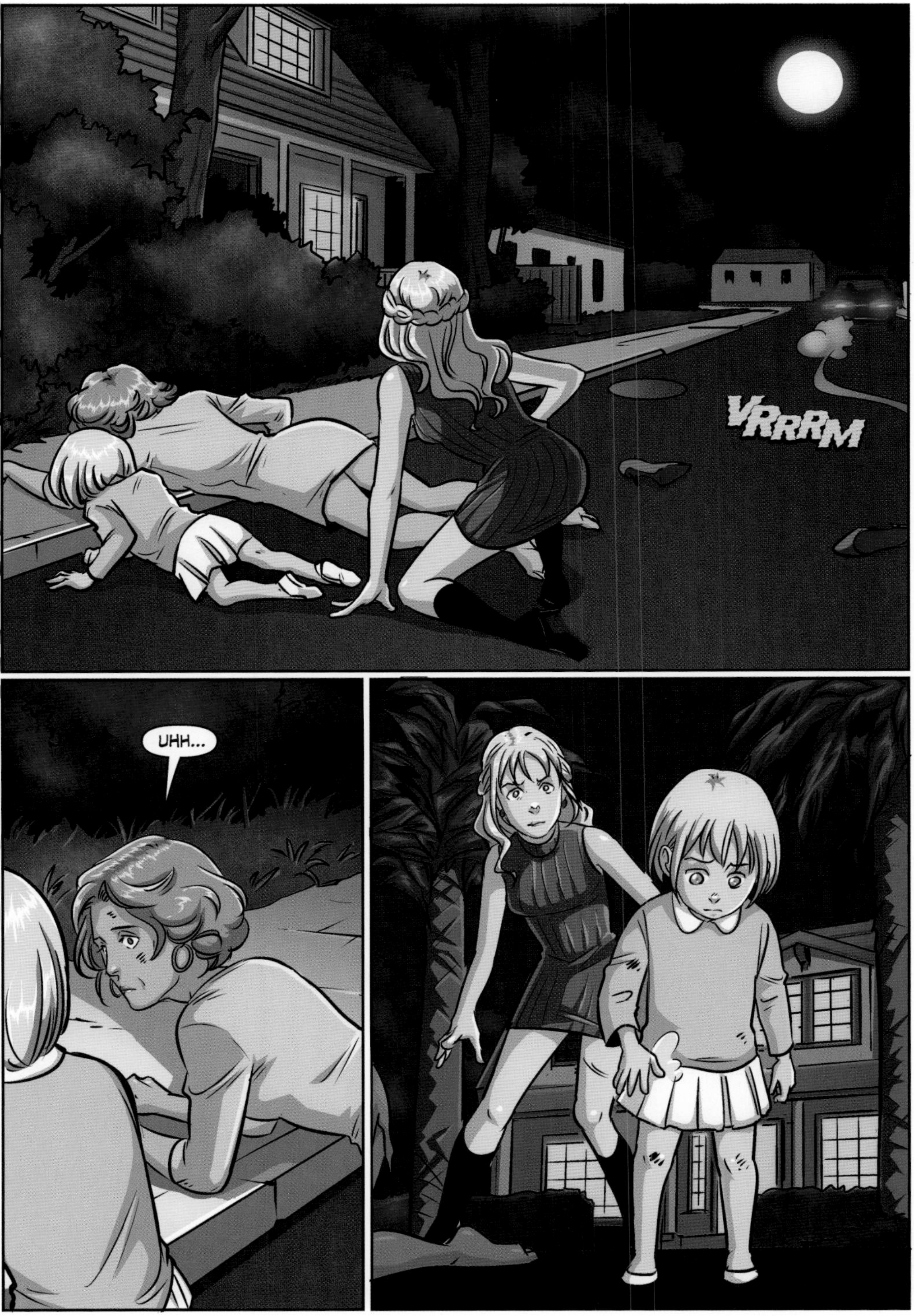
VRRRM
UHH...

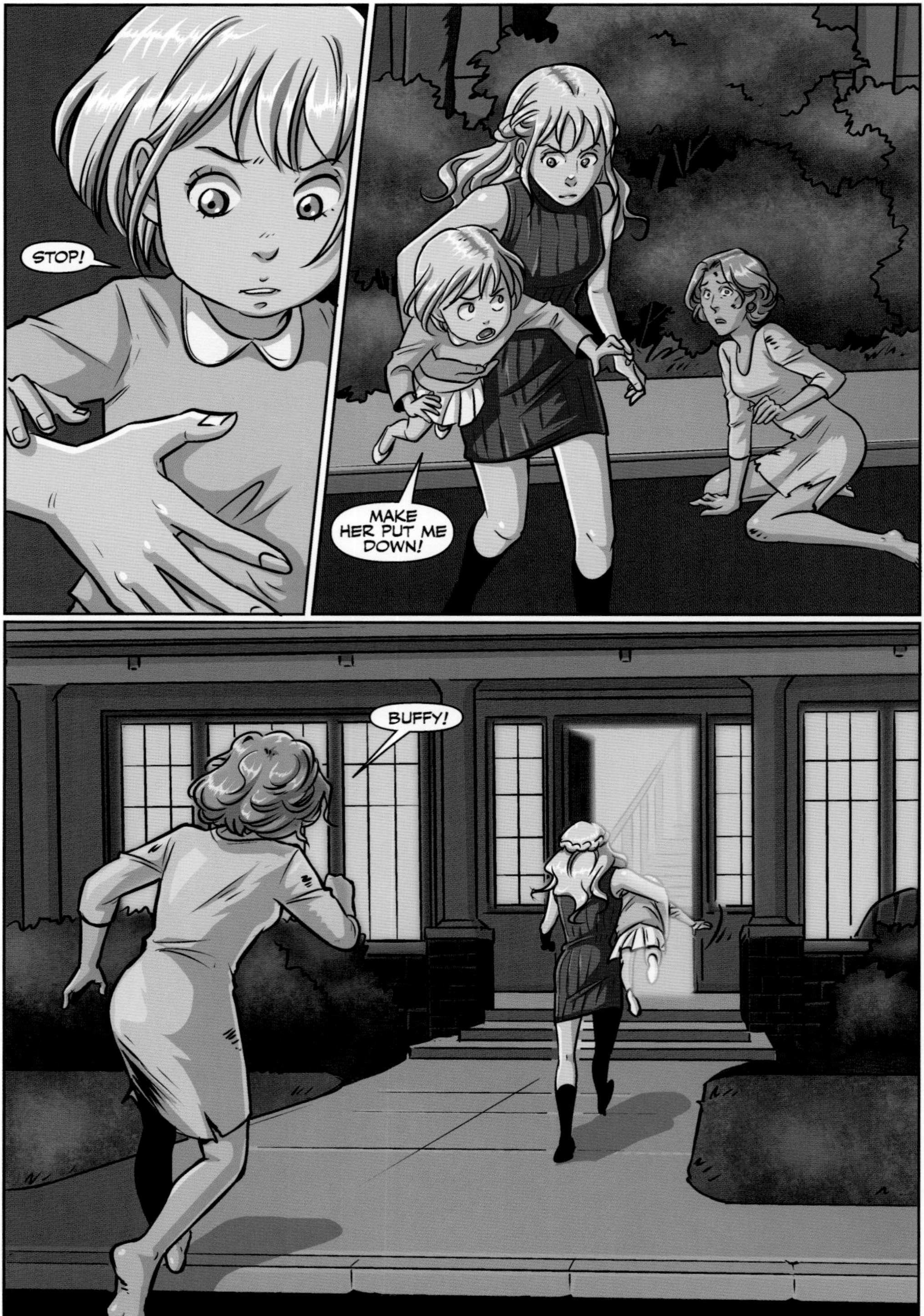
STOP!
MAKE HER PUT ME DOWN!
BUFFY!

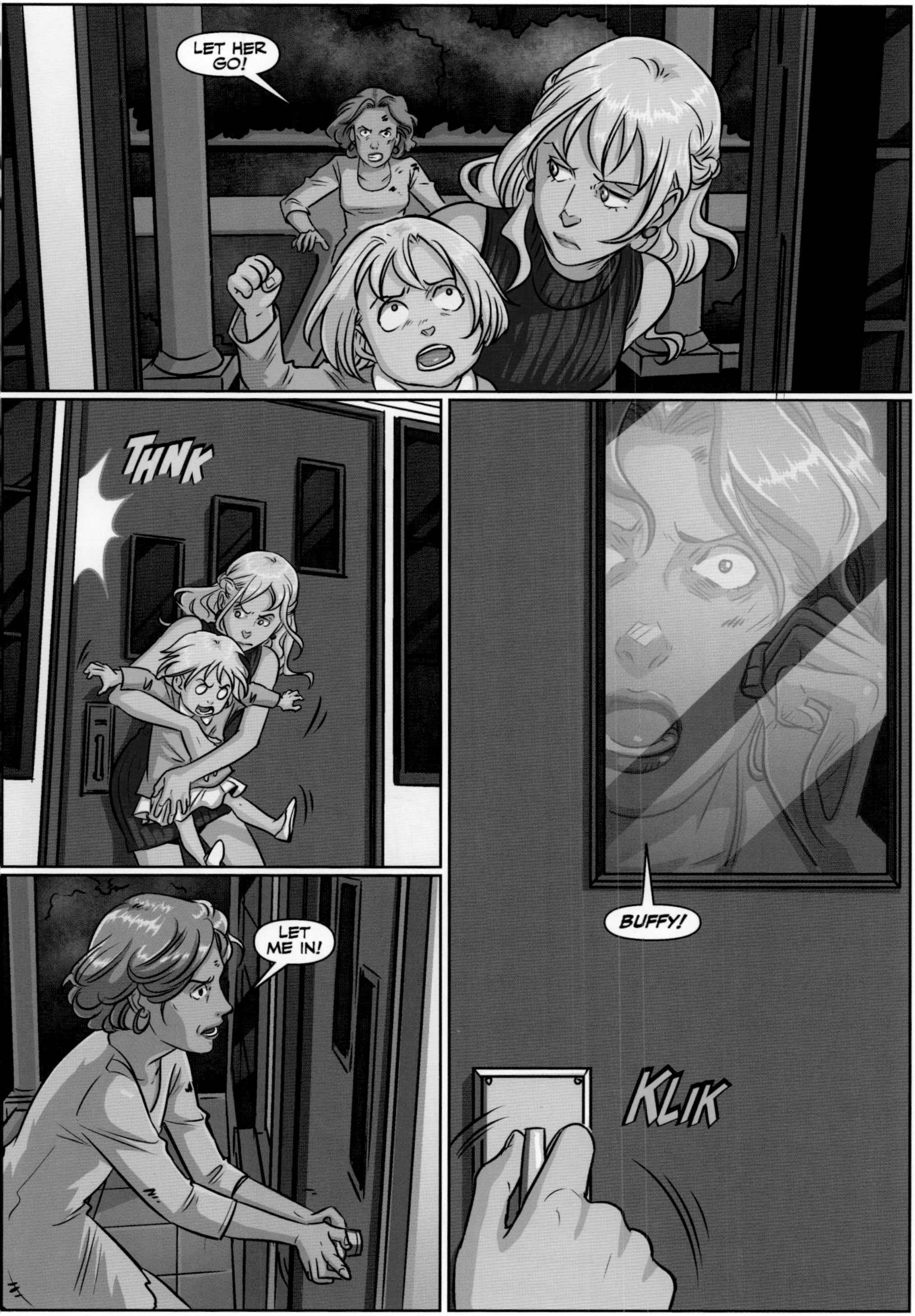
LET HER GO!
THNK
BUFFY!
LET ME IN!
KLIK

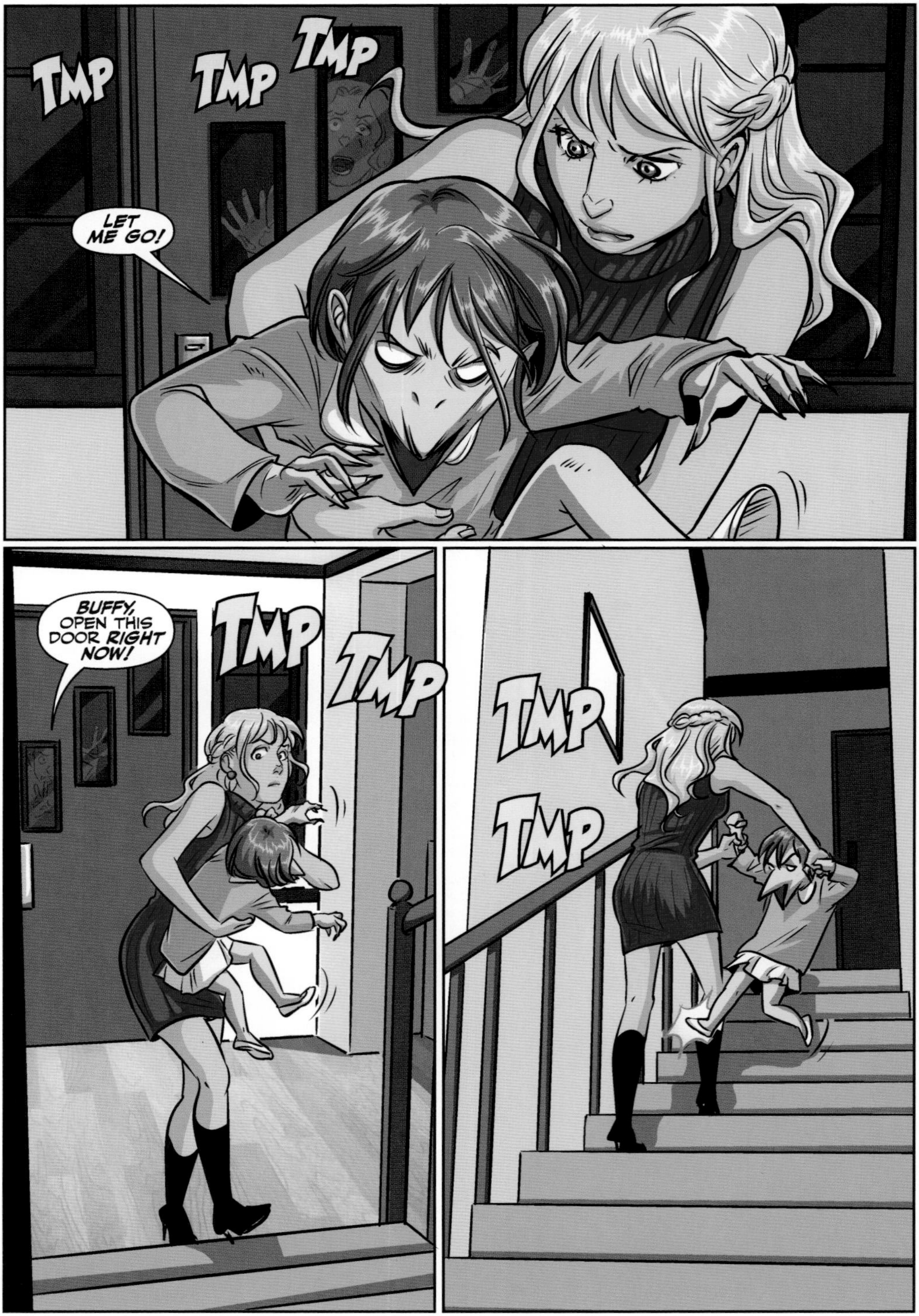
TMP
TMP
TMP
LET ME GO!
BUFFY, OPEN THIS DOOR RIGHT NOW!
TMP
TMP
TMP
TMP

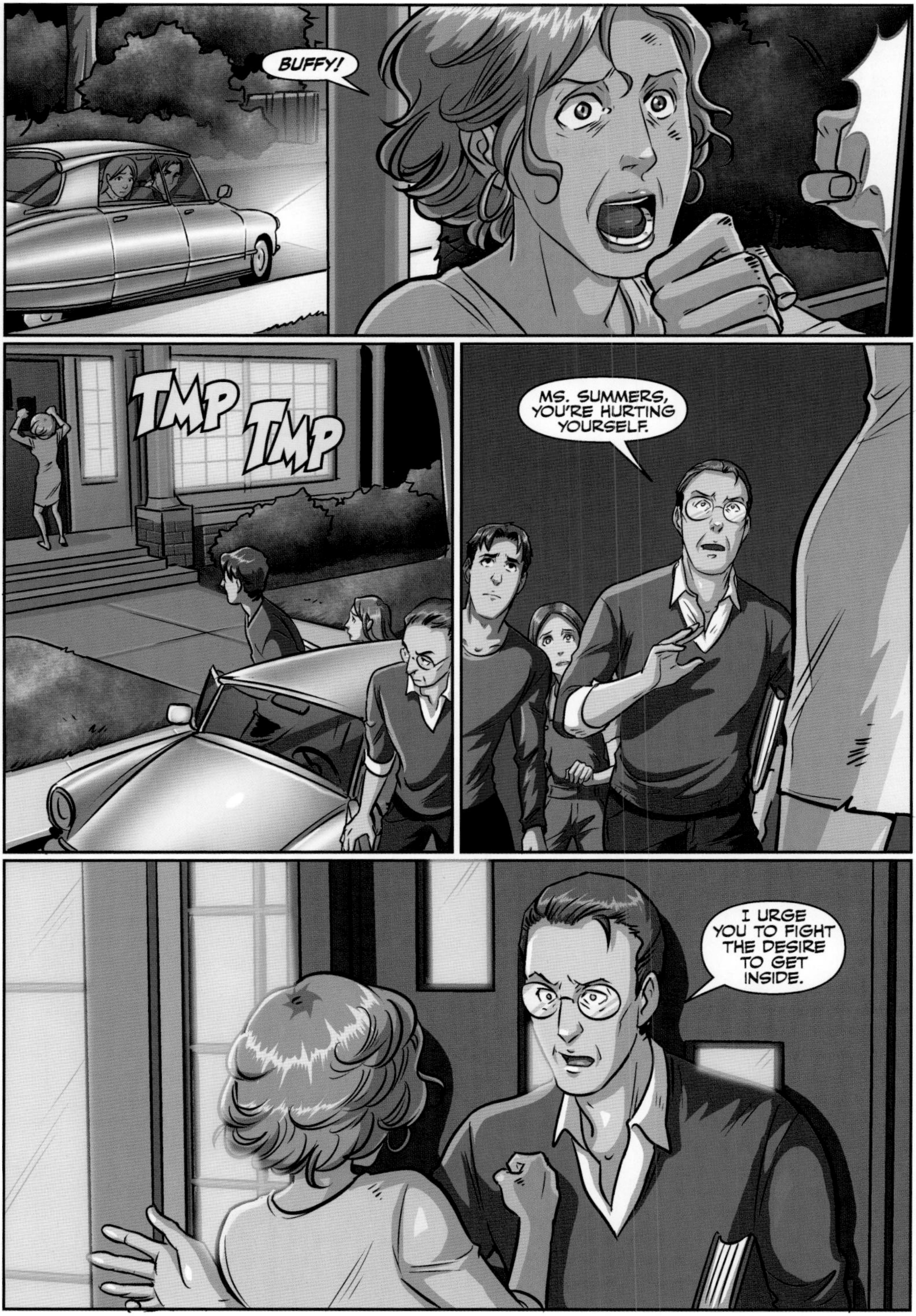
BUFFY!
TMP TMP
MS. SUMMERS, YOU'RE HURTING YOURSELF.
I URGE YOU TO FIGHT THE DESIRE TO GET INSIDE.

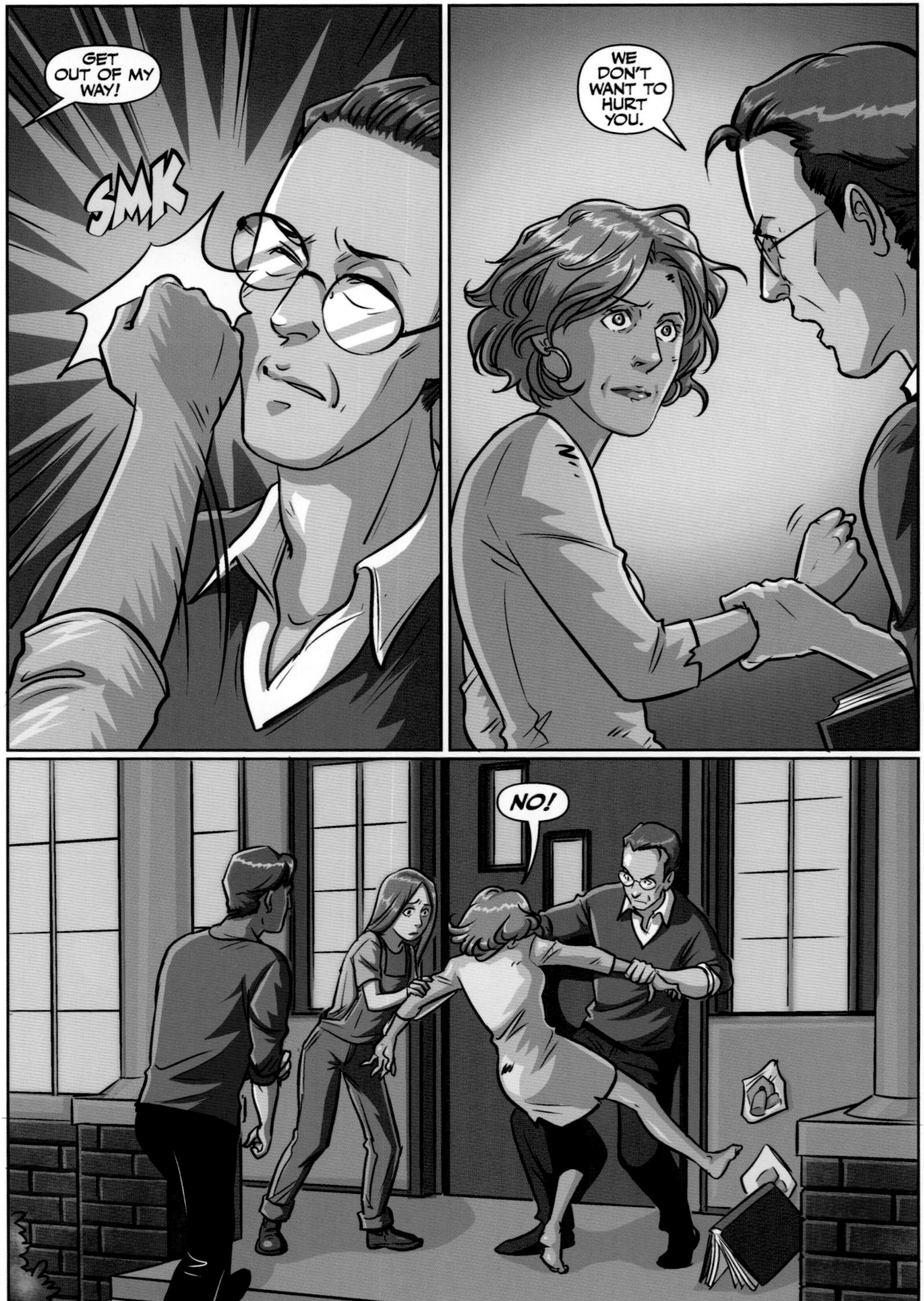
GET OUT OF MY WAY!
SMK
WE DON'T WANT TO HURT YOU.
NO!

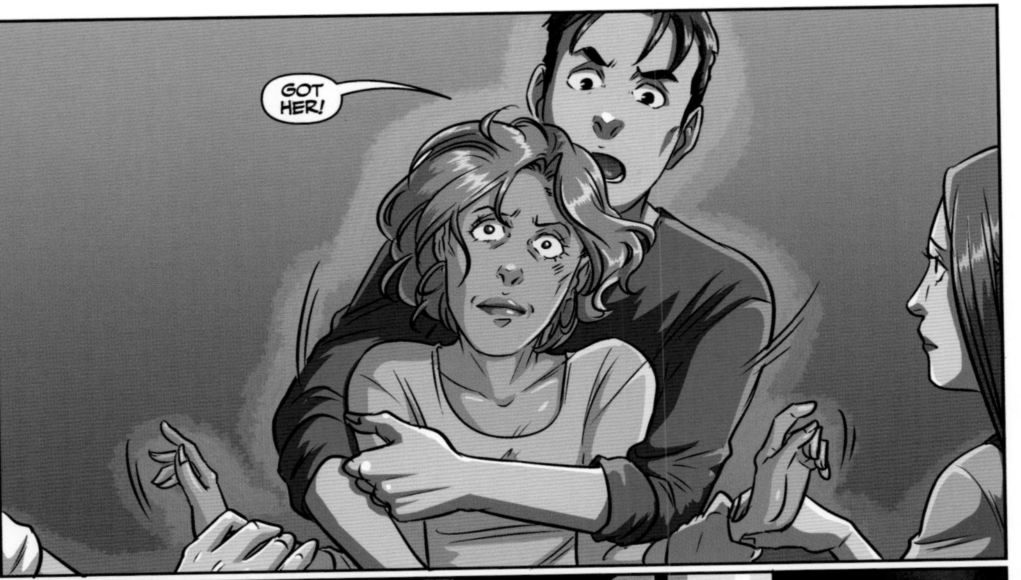
GOT HER!

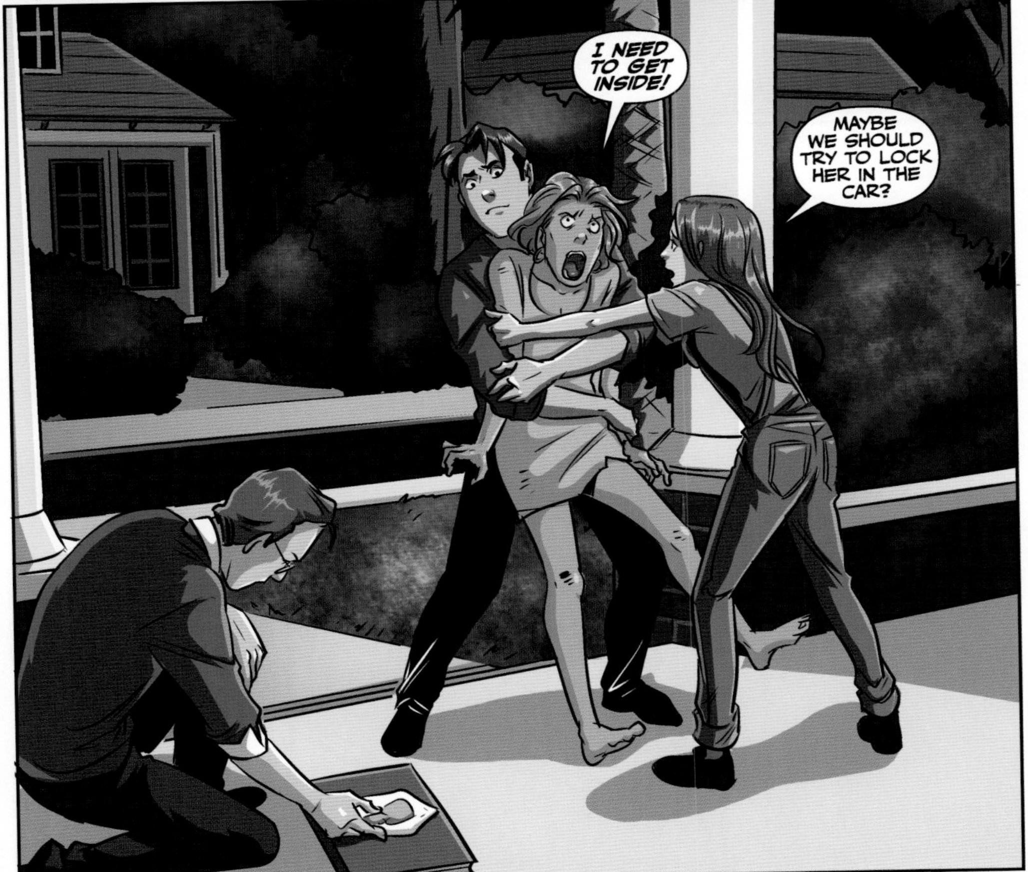
I NEED TO GET INSIDE!
MAYBE WE SHOULD TRY TO LOCK HER IN THE CAR?

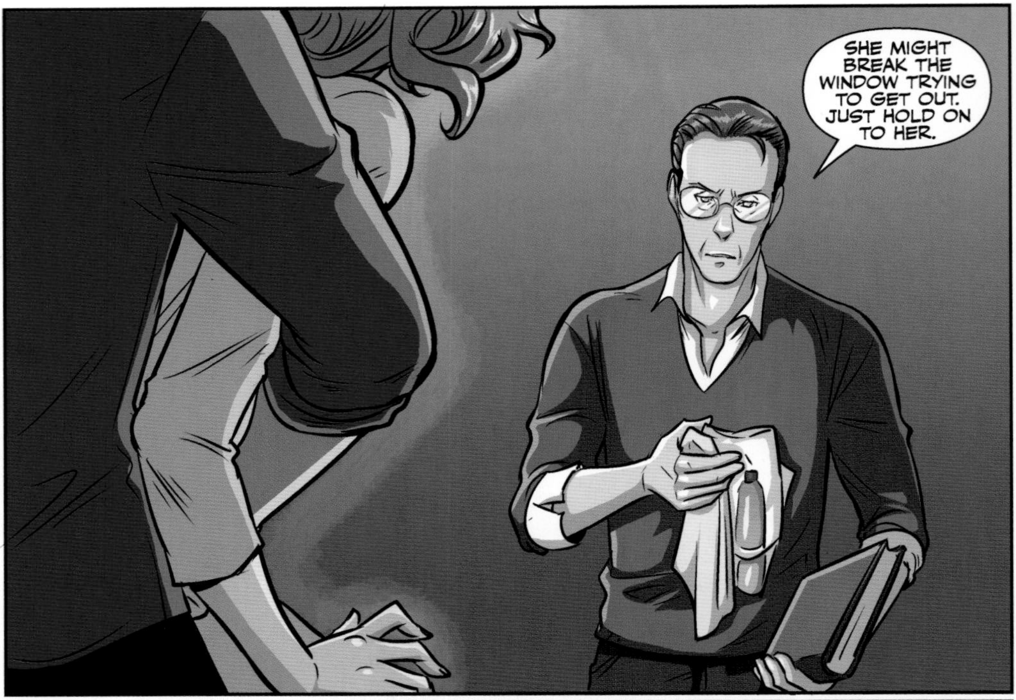
SHE MIGHT BREAK THE WINDOW TRYING TO GET OUT. JUST HOLD ON TO HER.

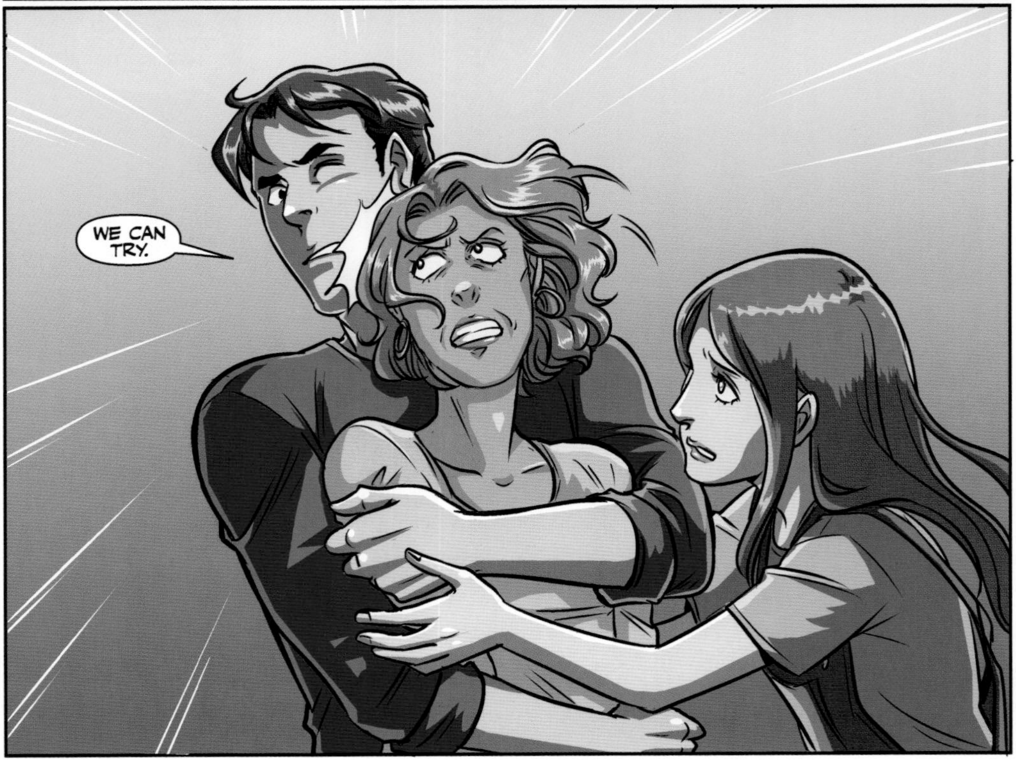
WE CAN TRY.

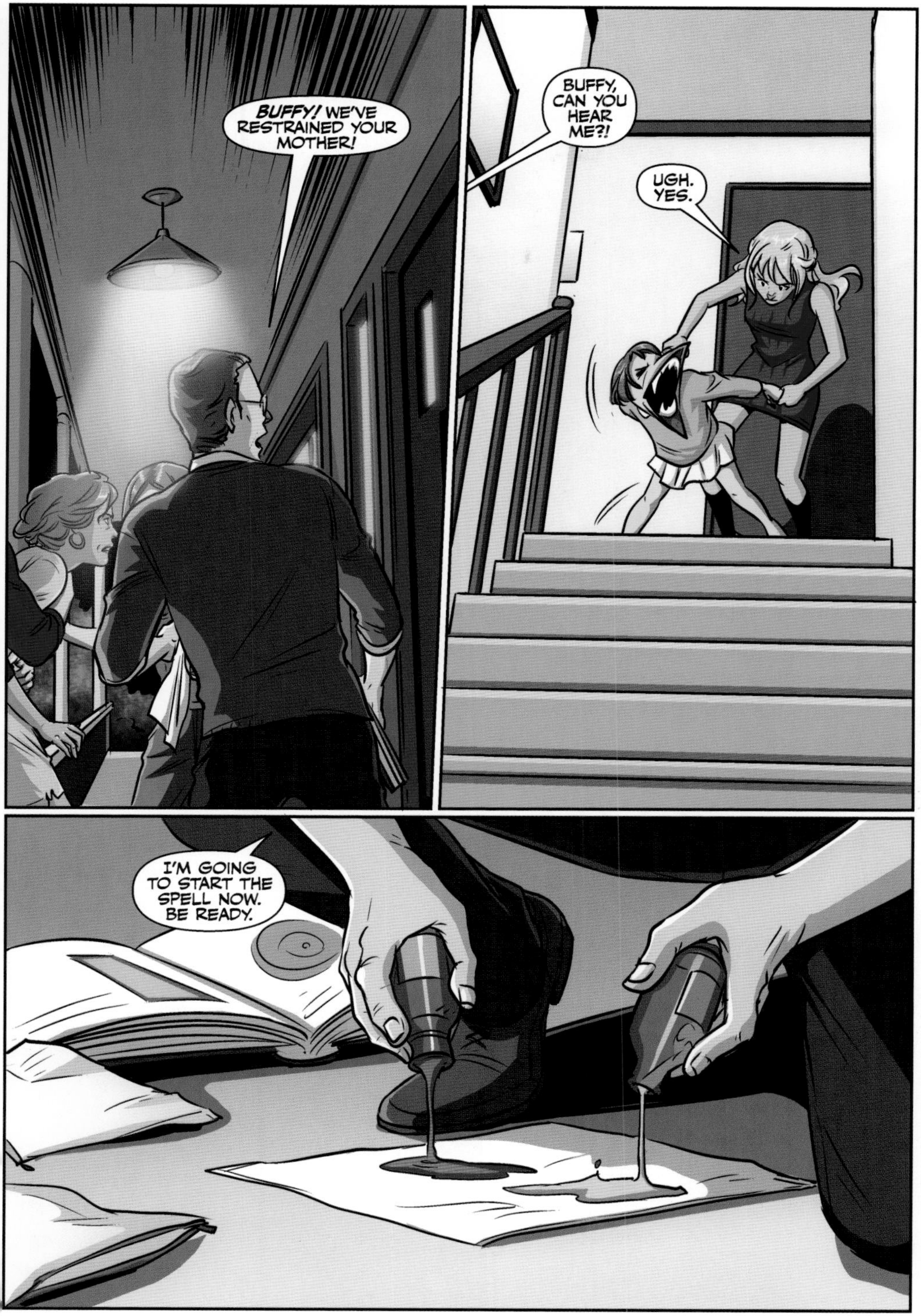
BUFFY! WE'VE RESTRAINED YOUR MOTHER!
BUFFY, CAN YOU HEAR ME?!
UGH. YES.
I'M GOING TO START THE SPELL NOW. BE READY.

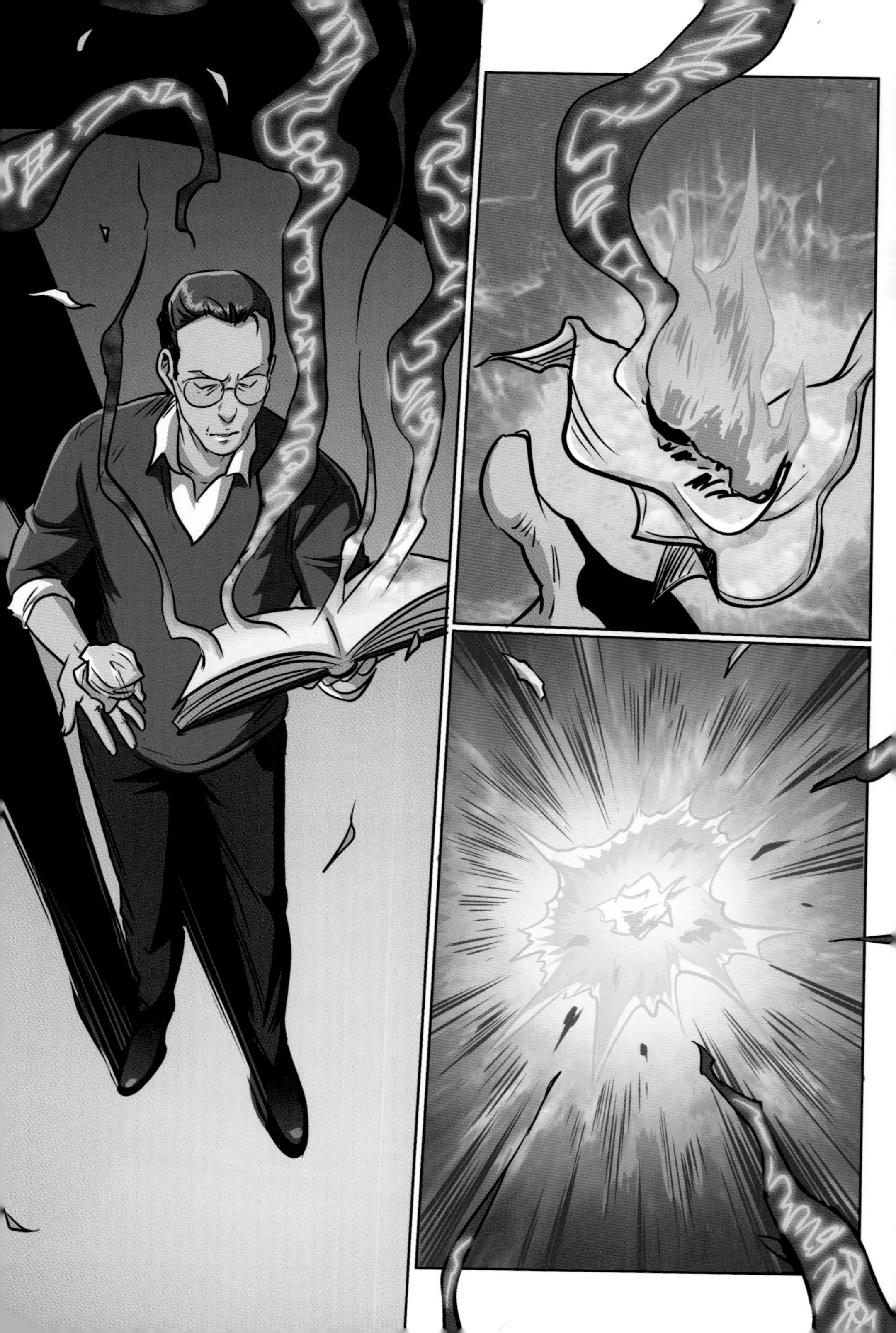

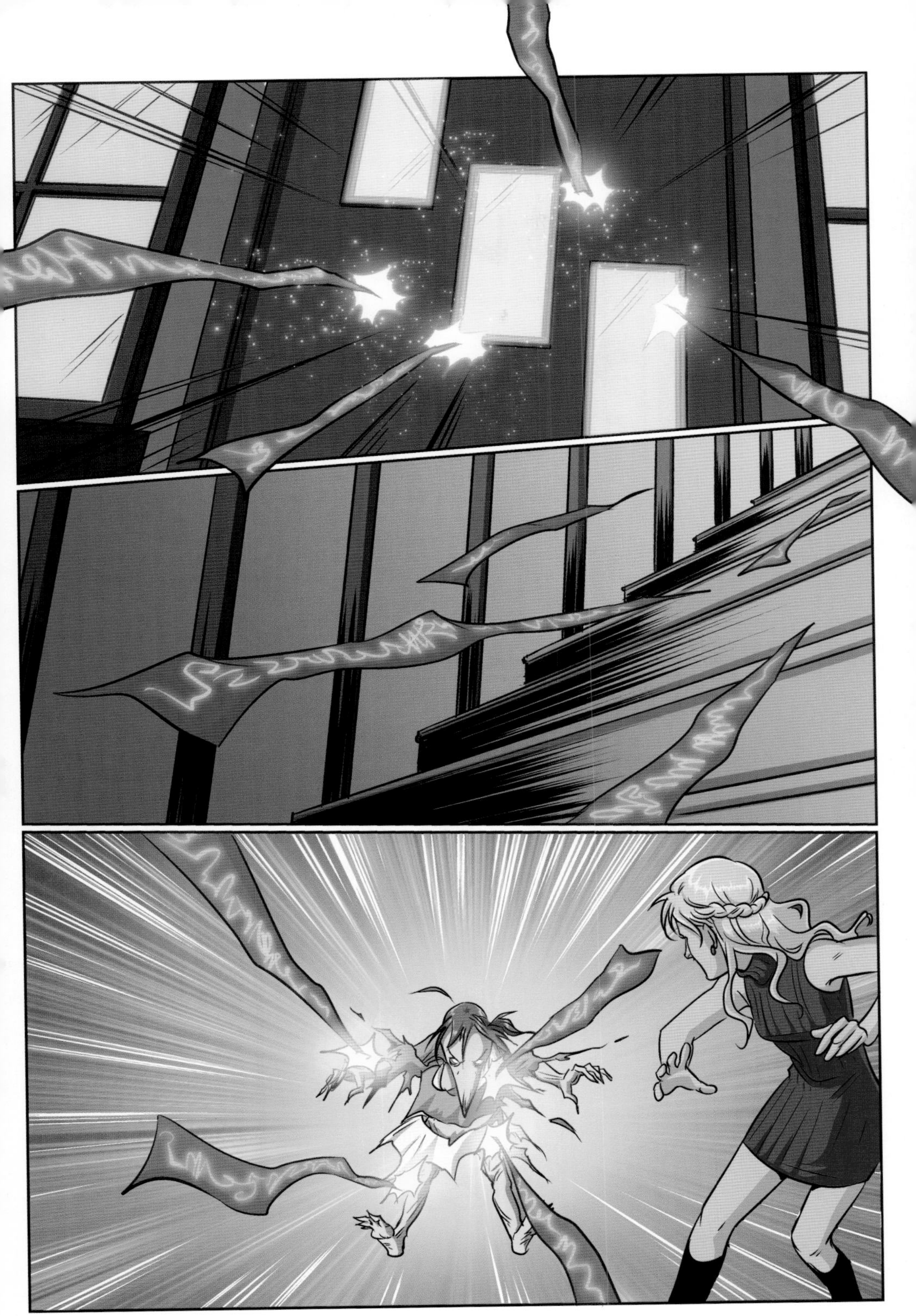

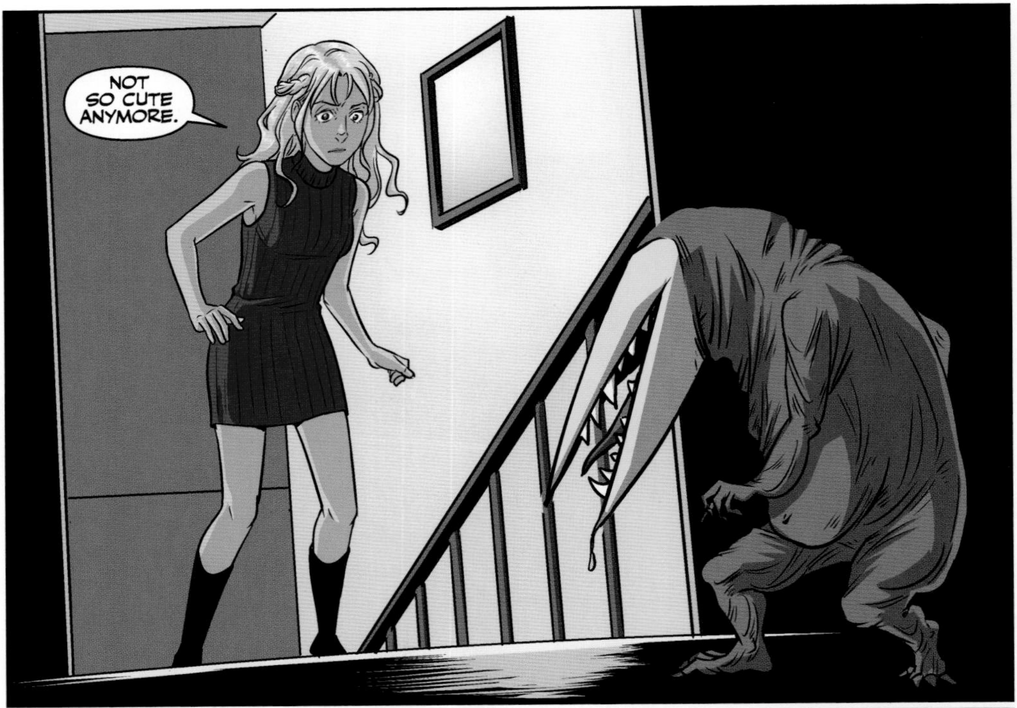
NOT SO CUTE ANYMORE.

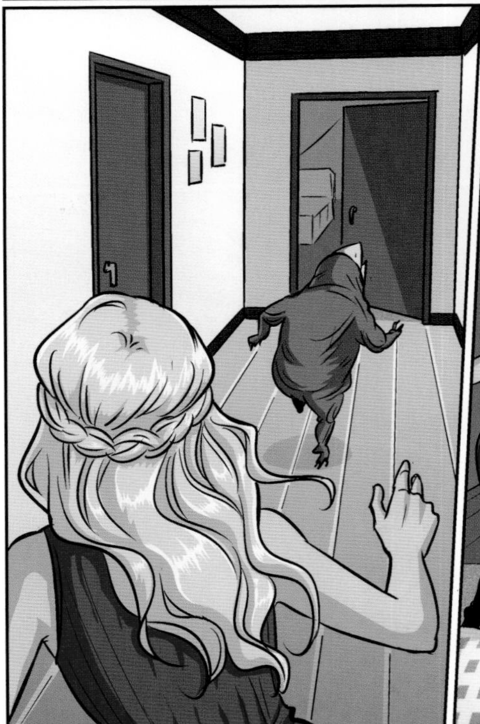

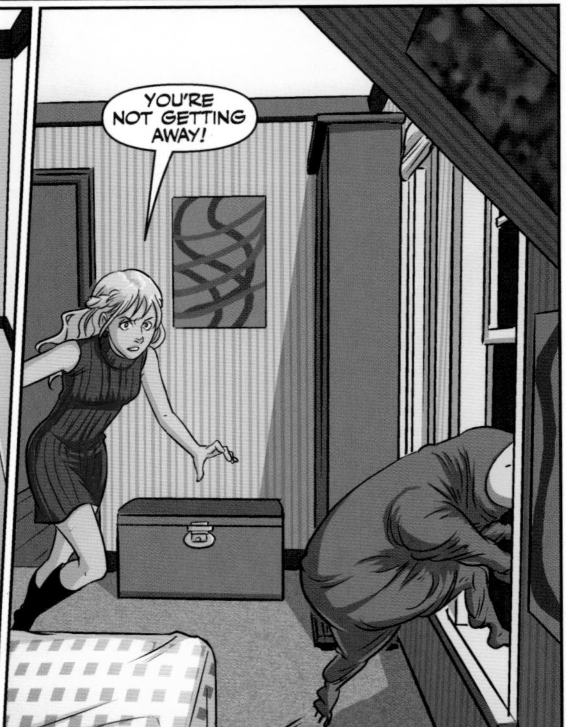
YOU'RE NOT GETTING AWAY!

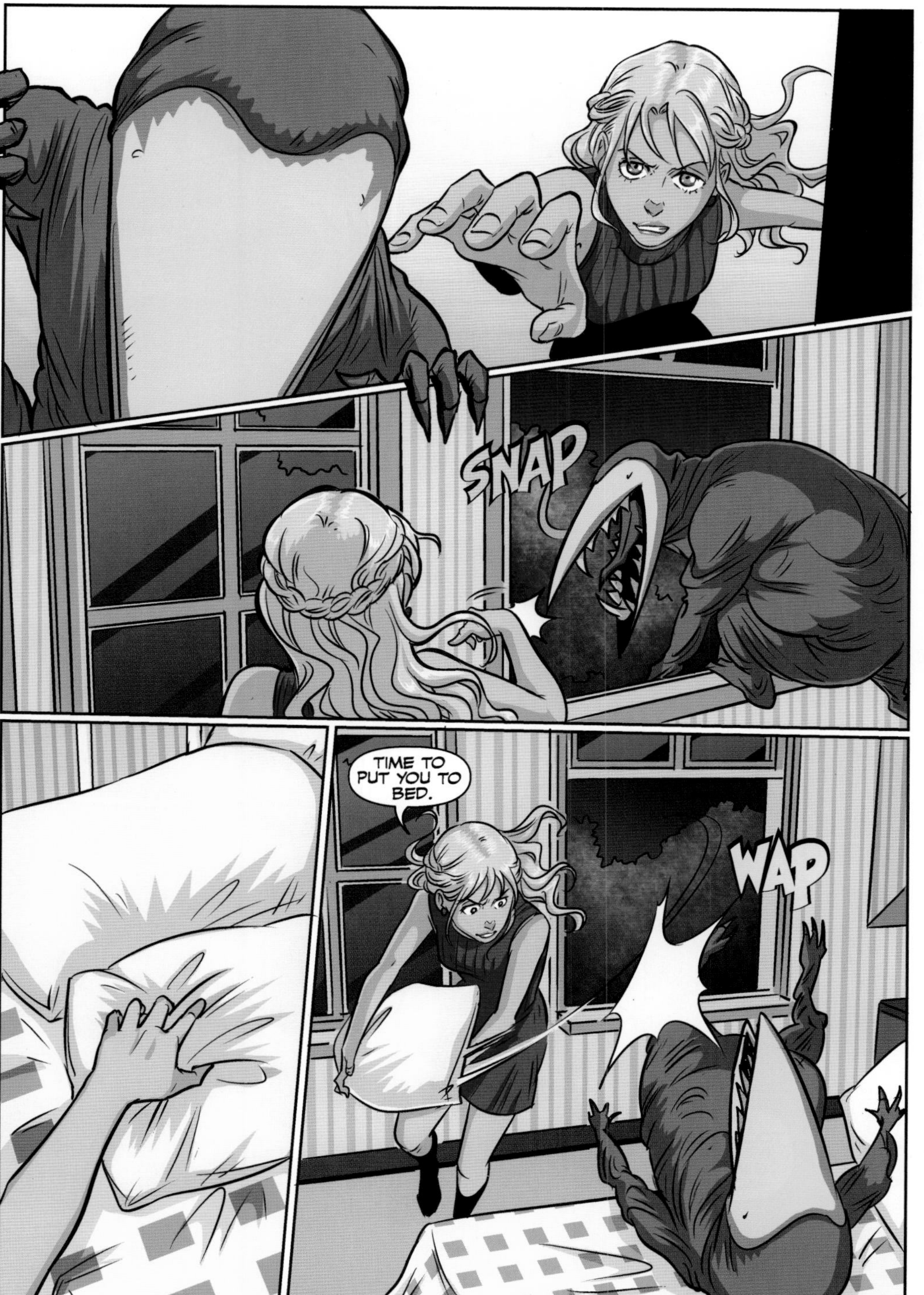
SNAP
TIME TO PUT YOU TO BED.
WAP

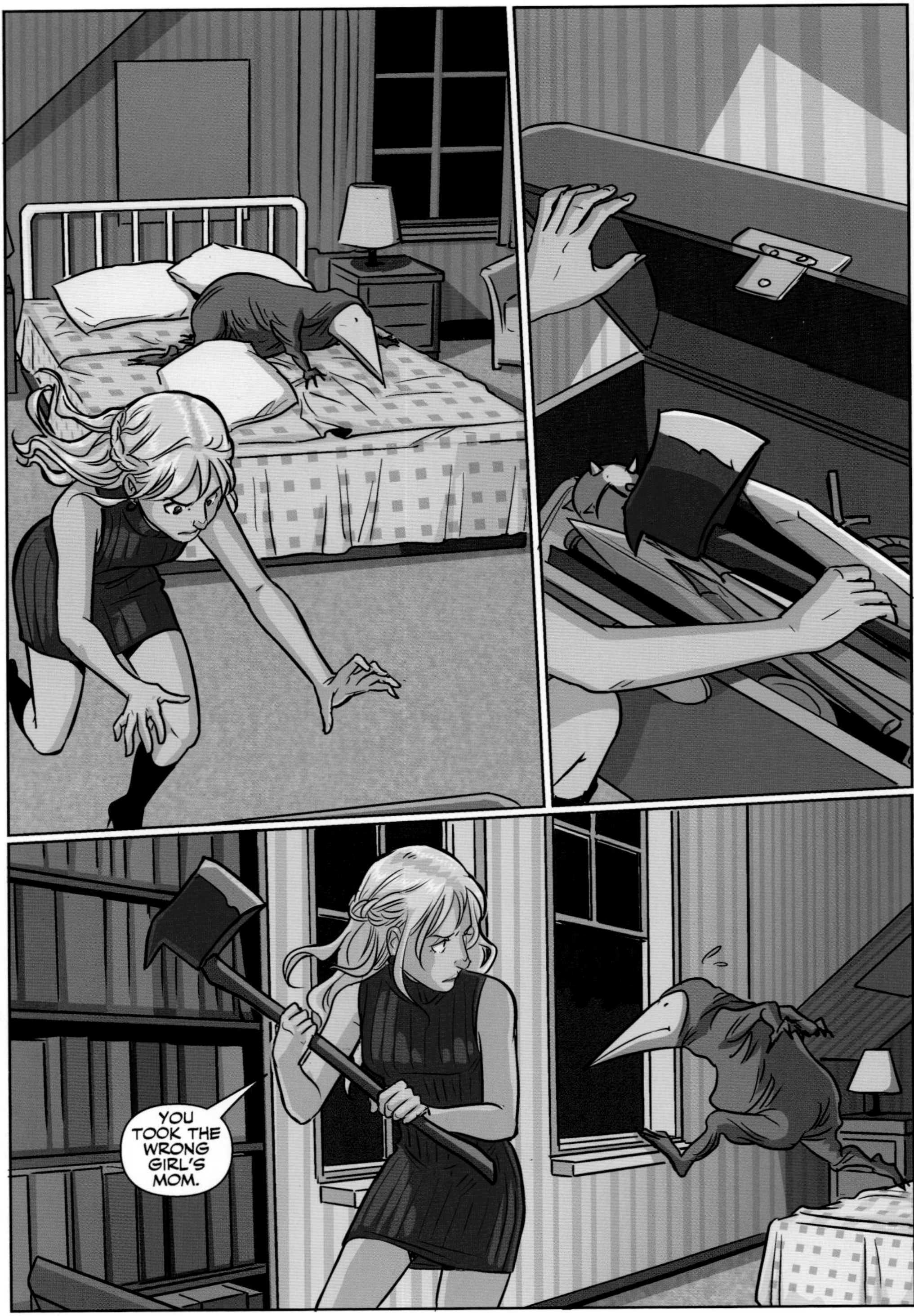
YOU TOOK THE WRONG GIRL'S MOM.

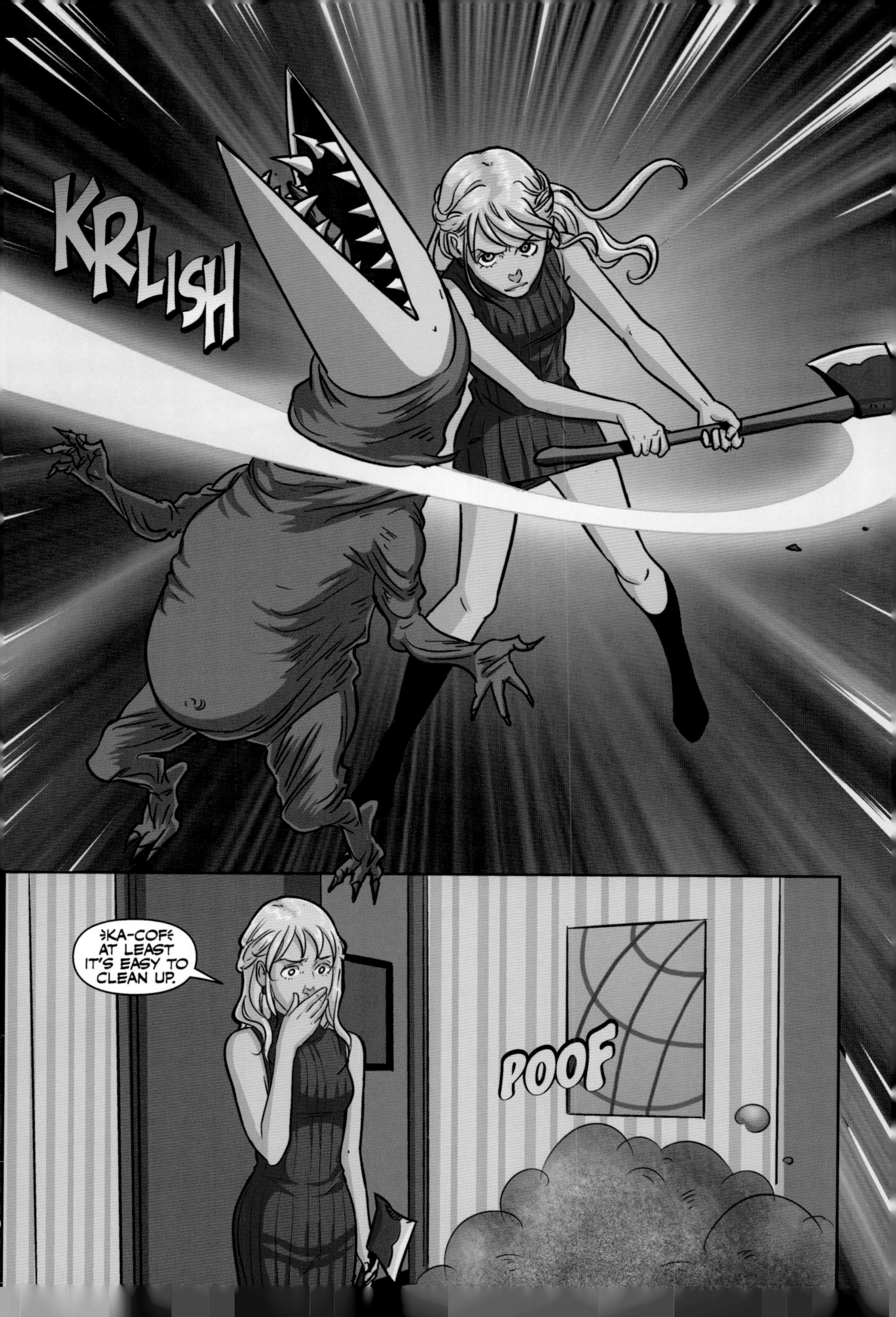
KRLISH
⁂KA-COF⁂ AT LEAST IT'S EASY TO CLEAN UP.
POOF

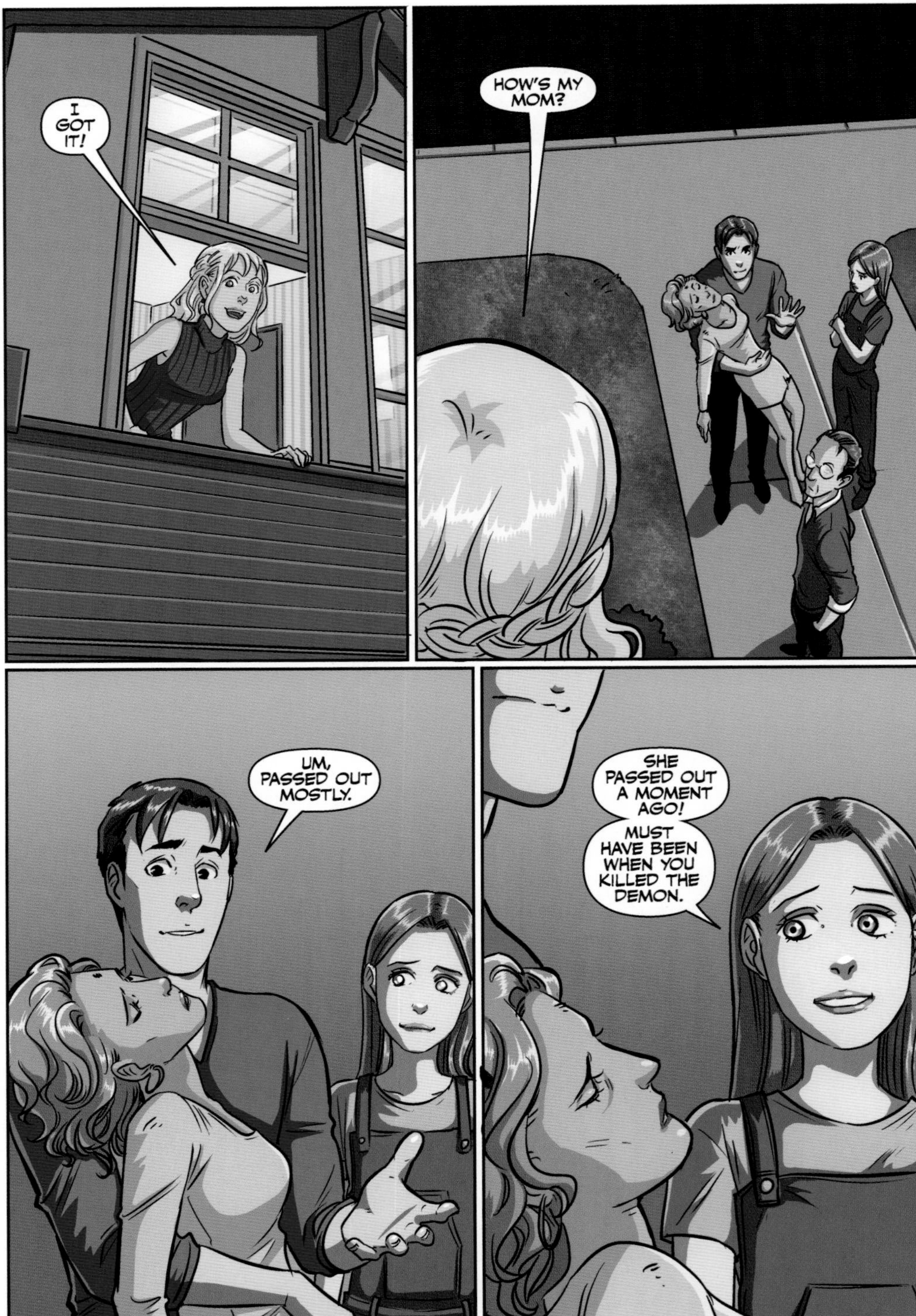
I GOT IT!
HOW'S MY MOM?
UM, PASSED OUT MOSTLY.
SHE PASSED OUT A MOMENT AGO!
MUST HAVE BEEN WHEN YOU KILLED THE DEMON.

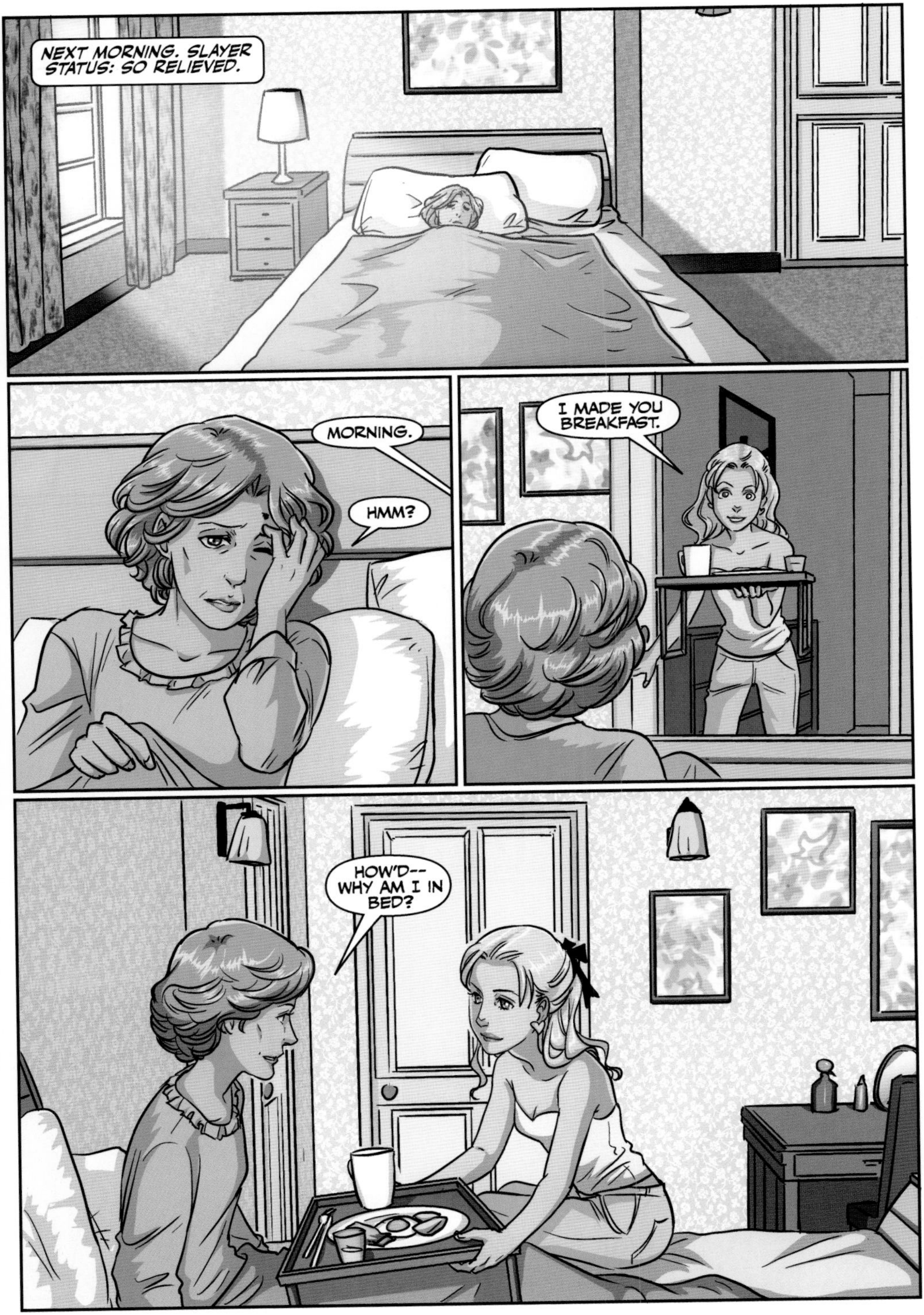

NEXT MORNING. SLAYER STATUS: SO RELIEVED.
MORNING.
HMM?
I MADE YOU BREAKFAST.
HOW'D-- WHY AM I IN BED?

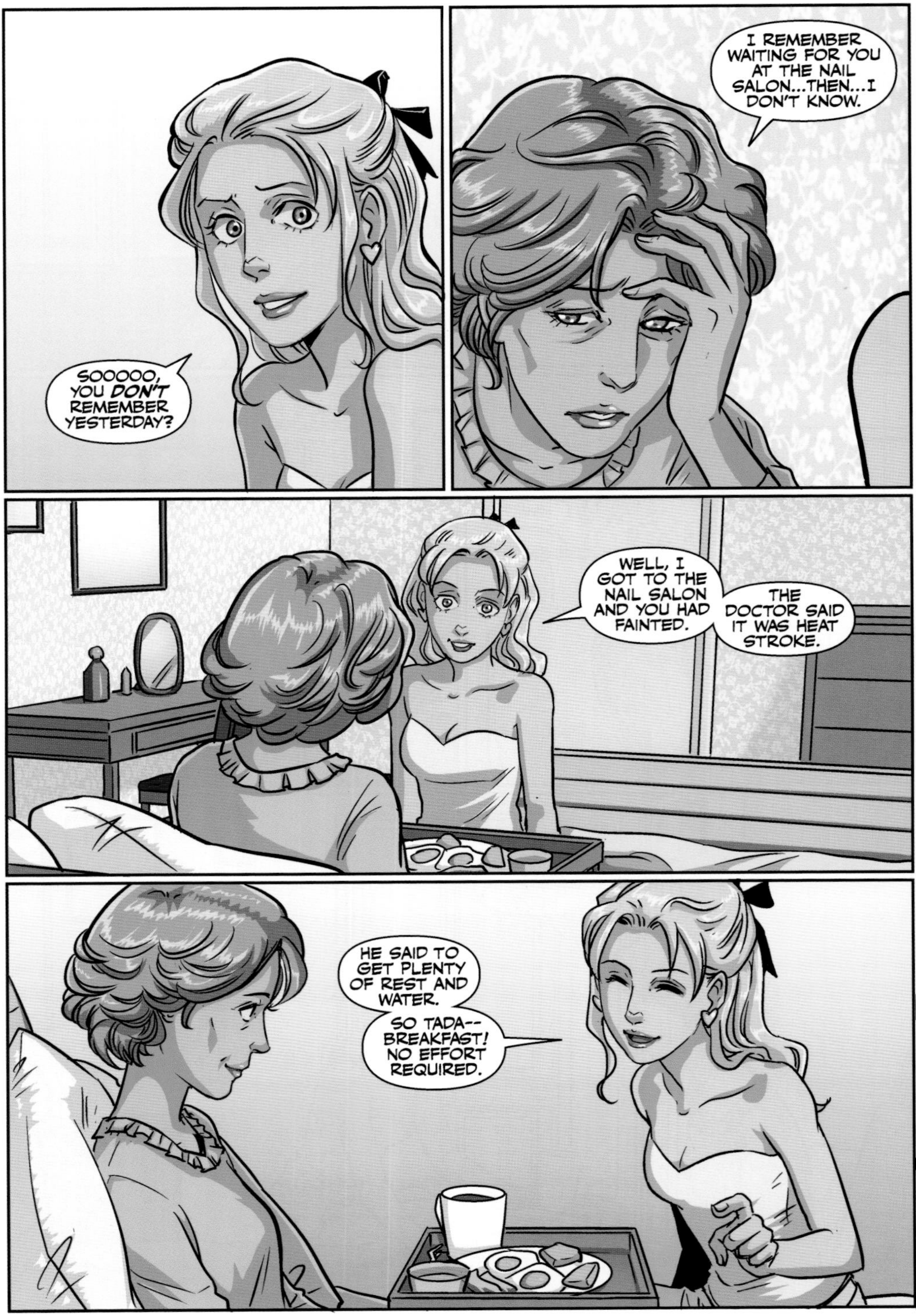
SOOOOO, YOU *DON'T* REMEMBER YESTERDAY?
I REMEMBER WAITING FOR YOU AT THE NAIL SALON...THEN...I DON'T KNOW.
WELL, I GOT TO THE NAIL SALON AND YOU HAD FAINTED.
THE DOCTOR SAID IT WAS HEAT STROKE.
HE SAID TO GET PLENTY OF REST AND WATER.
SO TADA-- BREAKFAST! NO EFFORT REQUIRED.

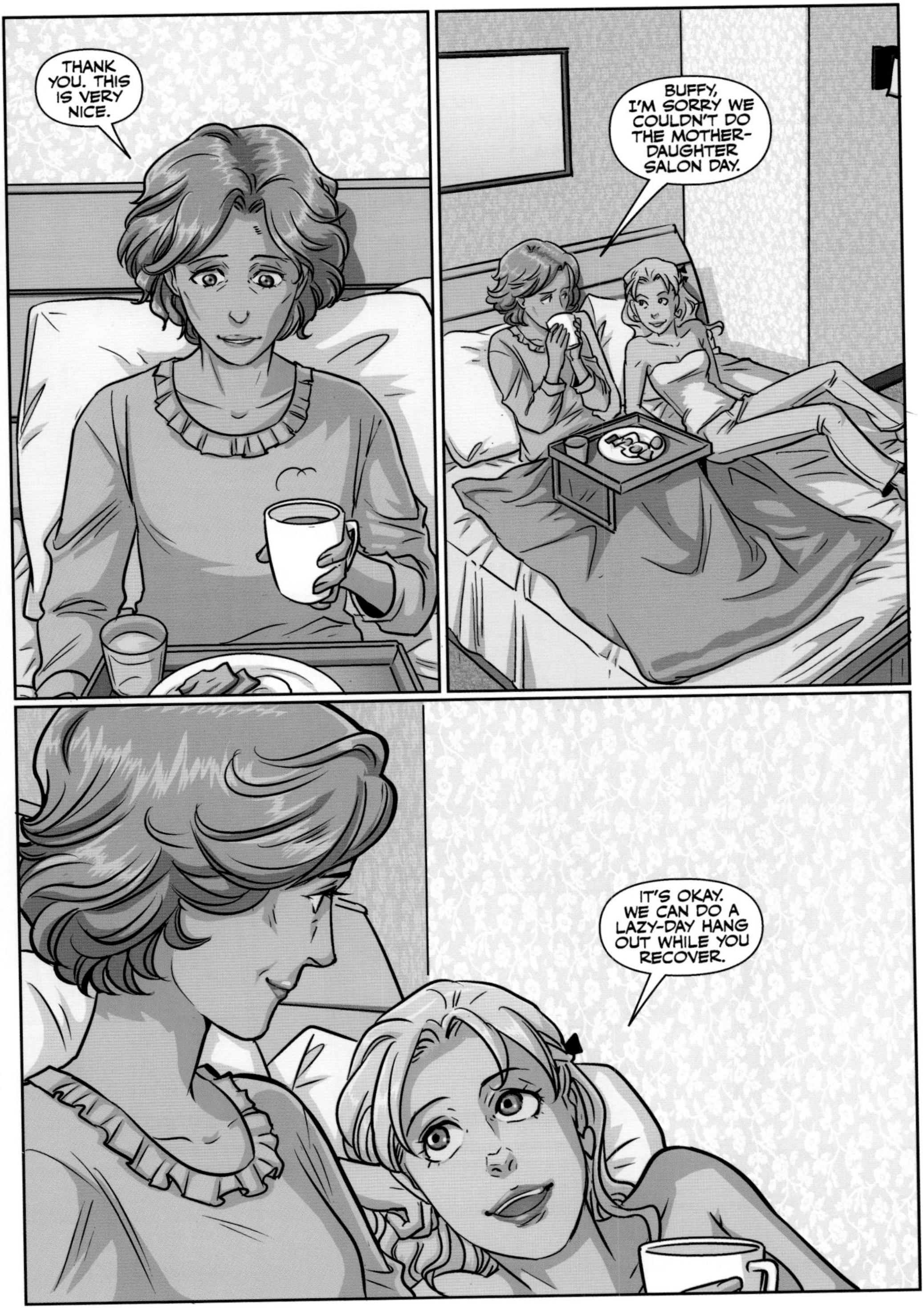
THANK YOU. THIS IS VERY NICE.
BUFFY, I'M SORRY WE COULDN'T DO THE MOTHER-DAUGHTER SALON DAY.
IT'S OKAY. WE CAN DO A LAZY-DAY HANG OUT WHILE YOU RECOVER.

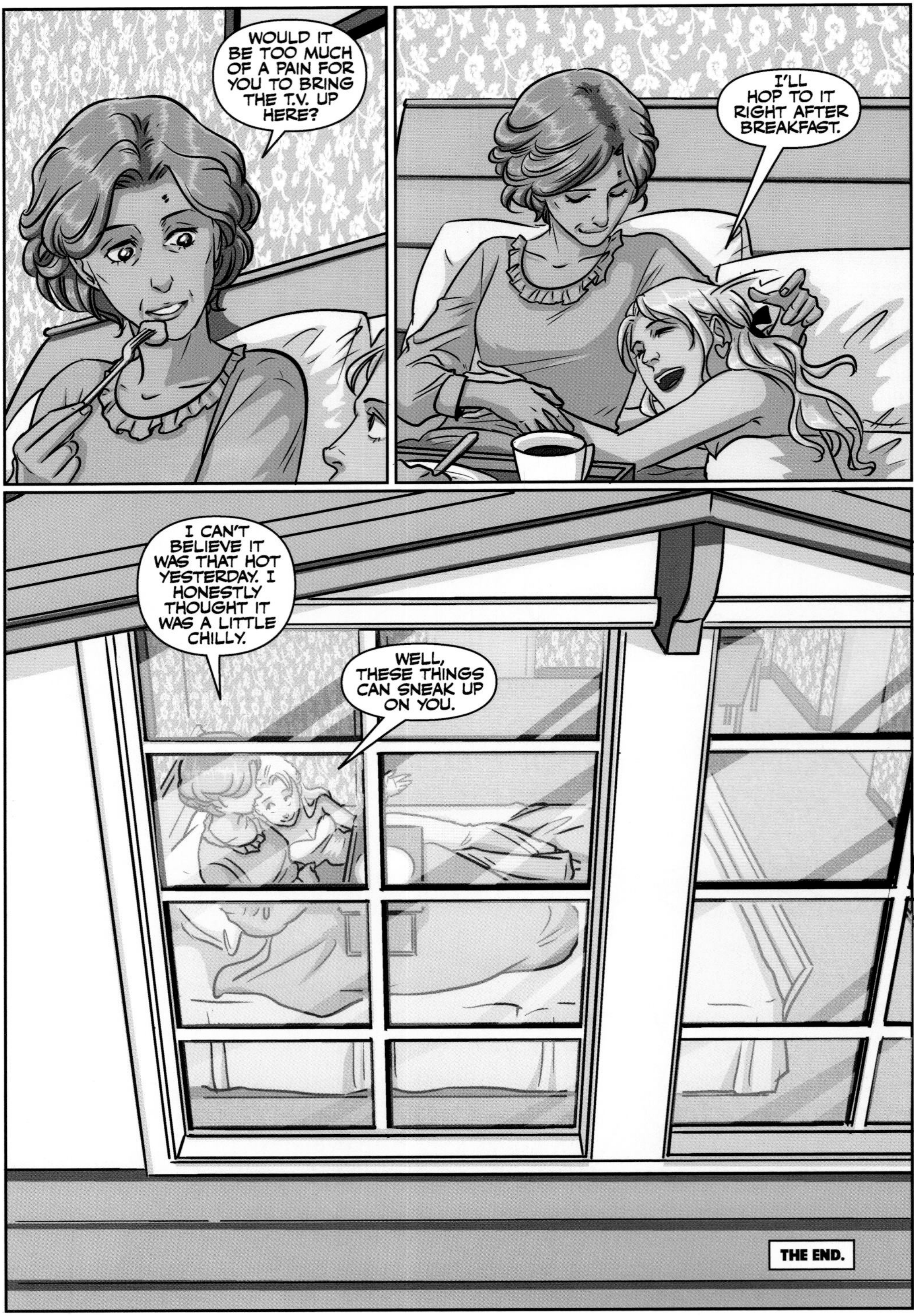
WOULD IT BE TOO MUCH OF A PAIN FOR YOU TO BRING THE T.V. UP HERE?
I'LL HOP TO IT RIGHT AFTER BREAKFAST.
I CAN'T BELIEVE IT WAS THAT HOT YESTERDAY. I HONESTLY THOUGHT IT WAS A LITTLE CHILLY.
WELL, THESE THINGS CAN SNEAK UP ON YOU.
THE END.